# ALMOST
# TOO
# LATE

# ALMOST TOO LATE

## Elmo Wortman

London
GEORGE ALLEN & UNWIN
Boston          Sydney

**George Allen & Unwin (Publishers) Ltd,
40 Museum Street, London WC1A 1LU, UK**

George Allen & Unwin (Publishers) Ltd,
Park Lane, Hemel Hempstead, Herts HP2 4TE, UK

Allen & Unwin Inc.,
9 Winchester Terrace, Winchester, Mass 01890, USA

George Allen & Unwin Australia Pty Ltd,
8 Napier Street, North Sydney, NSW 2060, Australia

First published in 1982

ISBN 0 04 910074 2

Printed in Great Britain
by Biddles Ltd, Guildford, Surrey

*Dedicated to Gran*

*We know that you worried.*
*You are the greatest, we love you.*

# Contents

# Publishers Note

American terminology has been kept in this edition because it is generally familiar to the British reader and because to change it would make the narrative, and especially the dialogue, seem artificial and stilted.

However, an explanation of certain trade names may be helpful, such as:

*Tang*—an orange-flavoured powder, mixed with water to make an instant orange juice.

*Cheez Whiz*—a cheese spread or paste.

*Pepto Bismol*—a liquid medicine for indigestion and other stomach complaints.

# Acknowledgments

Our thanks go to Nels and Patty Soderstrom, in appreciation of their assistance in taping interviews and conversations when we were just out of the hospital, and for the many hours they gave to transcribe those tapes, to determine our technical accuracy and to assist in the early writing efforts. Without their attention to detail this book could never be as complete nor reflect our experience so accurately.

# ALMOST
# TOO
# LATE

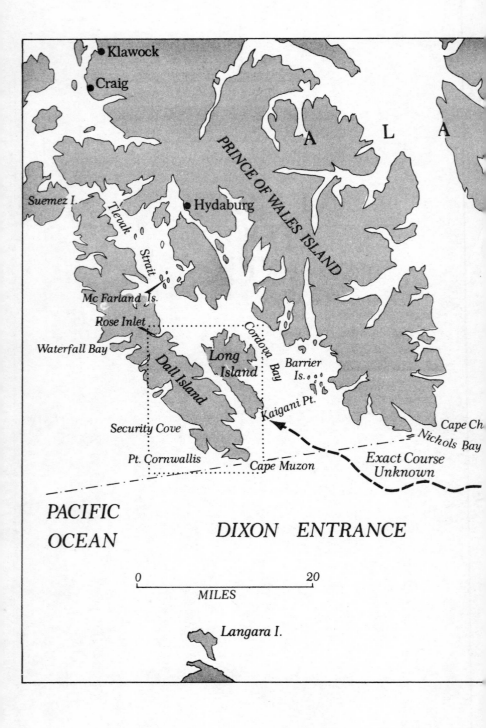

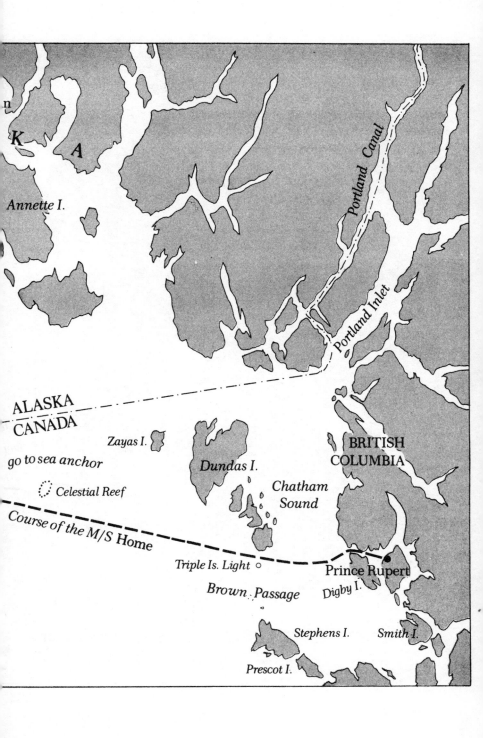

# Voyage from Long Island to Dall Island

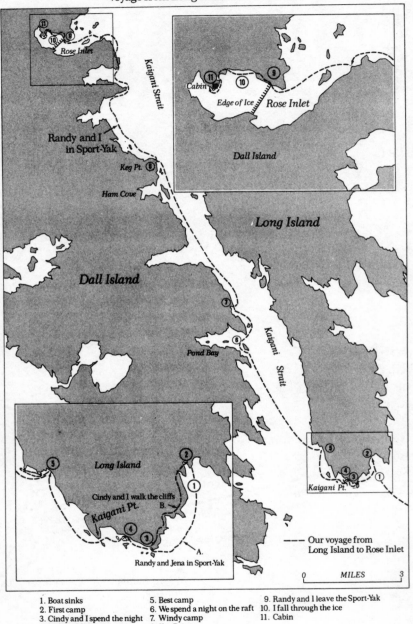

Kaigani Strait

Randy and I
in Sport-Yak

Keg Pt.

Ham Cove

Rose Inlet

Cabin

Edge of Ice

Rose Inlet

Dall Island

Long Island

Dall Island

Kaigani Strait

Pond Bay

Long Island

Cindy and I walk the cliffs

B.

Kaigani Pt.

A.

Randy and Jena in Sport-Yak

Kaigani Pt.

— — — Our voyage from
Long Island to Rose Inlet

0        MILES        3

1. Boat sinks
2. First camp
3. Cindy and I spend the night
4. Raft-building camp
5. Best camp
6. We spend a night on the raft
7. Windy camp
8. Keg Point
9. Randy and I leave the Sport-Yak
10. I fall through the ice
11. Cabin

# Prologue

WE didn't plan to be away very long, but in the turbulent waters of Dixon Entrance in February, one's plans are often altered by a violent and unforgiving Mother Nature. This happens regularly, even to ships and barges that are much larger and better equipped than our thirty-three-foot sailboat and that are manned by professional crews.

The mouth of Dixon Entrance opens wide to the violent storms and relentless swells of the north Pacific Ocean. Here tidal currents that feed and release the waters of more sheltered bays, inlets, straits and channels of northern British Columbia and southeast Alaska surge in and out with strength and regularity. These conditions make the weather changeable and hard to predict. In addition, the east-west boundary line between the United States and Canada passes the length of the entrance, so it is difficult to get a comprehensive weather report from either country. In eleven previous crossings, we learned to rely on weather forecasts only for the location of major storm centers. We had to go to Dixon Entrance in person to determine local conditions.

Our boat, the *Home,* was small for water that can be so rough, but it was sturdy. The children and I built it ourselves, and the five of us—Margery, Cindy, Randy, Jena and I—had been sailing it together for about four years in these northwest coastal waters. During that time, the *Home* had performed well, and her family crew rapidly gained experience and skills—skills that were soon to be tested to the limit.

First, some words to explain why we were in the boat harbor at Prince Rupert, British Columbia, on that winter afternoon. I am Elmo Wortman: age, fifty-two; divorced father of four; occupation, carpenter—at least until a few years ago, when rheumatic problems started making my work increasingly difficult. Soon I was unable to keep abreast of the other workers, then unable even to hold a job. It turned out I had *ankylosing spondylitis*, a rheumatic illness of the back, neck, arms and shoulders. "Incurable," the doctors said. "Stay home and care for the children. Take aspirin. No physical exertion. Social Security."

I was only forty-eight when this life sentence was passed. The children had been with me for four years and were then about thirteen, eleven, ten and eight. We were living in Washington State and had the sailboat near completion, except for masts and rigging. For two years, any money that was not needed immediately for food, clothes or a roof over our heads had gone into building it. Perhaps I should say that the boat came first whenever I had a paycheck. We managed to get by on what was left. Hoping that perhaps just a few months of rest might improve my condition, I did not apply for Social Security disability benefits immediately. Instead, I went to the children's schools and got textbooks, and we loaded everything we owned aboard our new *Home* and motored about five hundred miles north to the coast of British Columbia. Though on about the same latitude as Calgary and Winnipeg, we now had much milder winter temperatures, because of the moderating effect of the Japanese current. This same influence also kept summertime temperatures low. The water was always too cold for comfortable swimming.

By living away from centers of population, we got by with what we had and what we could find in the wilds. There was almost no money, but we harvested plenty of food from the beaches, tidelands and waters. We located a good shrimp bed and kept a pot in it that provided two or three pounds daily. We searched for and found good fishing for red snapper, cod and scallops. We lived near excellent clam beaches. The children's coats seldom had all their buttons. Their socks never matched. I tried to keep them in boots without holes in the bottoms but was not always successful. Barnacles and light rubber boots are incompatible.

We needed a few staples—flour, rice, seasonings—and gasoline for the small outboard motor we used on our skiff. If we happened to have $100 for the month, we used it all. If we only had $10, we made it do. Survival was not something we read about or prepared for; it was what we lived daily. The children loved it, and I preferred it to the food stamps, rent subsidies and welfare that would have been our life had we remained in civilization.

To get more room than we had aboard the boat, I built a twelve-by-thirty-three-foot cabin on piling on one of the isolated beaches. The materials came from drift piles, reclaimed lumber from an abandoned shed at an old logging site and poles that we cut and peeled in the forest. The children helped, doing most of the heavier work. The job was a slow, laborious and painful one, but it moved steadily to completion.

In April 1975, when we knew the highest tides of the year were approaching, we found large spruce logs on the beaches and moved them near our cabin, an operation that required little effort other than judicious use of time and tide. Then, as the highest of the tides flooded into the little lagoon, we maneuvered the logs into place lengthwise under the cabin while the incoming tide performed its carefully planned part in the show by setting the whole thing adrift, and our floathouse appeared, center stage, entire cast receiving a well-deserved curtain call. (Well, we can at least pretend that someone saw us in this hour of triumph.)

From that time on, the floathouse was our main living center, providing us with a small living area. The sailboat was tied alongside to furnish storage space, bedrooms and an electric supply when needed. Although our living space was limited, our front yard stretched as far as the eye could see. And if the view got dull, we could change it on short notice.

Social Security disability benefits had by now been applied for, the physical examinations, red tape and a several-month waiting period complied with, and we were receiving a monthly check. This new affluence—by our standards—helped me confront problems I had tried to overlook when we had too few dollars to face them squarely. Cindy needed orthodontia work badly, Randy and Jena to a lesser degree. The children had had no public schooling for two years. We were aliens in Canada. It seemed best to return to the United States and get our act together.

I wanted to load our gear aboard the boat and move down the coast to southern California. The kids all enjoyed swimming, and the warmer weather would be a welcome change. They outvoted me, however, and opted for southeast Alaska, more than five hundred miles to the north. We had lived in Alaska when Randy and Jena were born. Margery and Cindy could not remember back beyond it. It would be like going home for all of them.

We decided to try to take the floathouse with us, pulling it by the boat with its small diesel engine. If for any reason we should be unsuccessful, it could be committed to the drift piles it came from, while we put our belongings on the sailboat and continued our journey.

The gods smiled on us; or perhaps they were laughing. Twenty-one days later, we were tied to the beach near Craig, Alaska, on the west side of Prince of Wales Island. From there, Margery and Cindy went to the high school in Craig; Randy and Jena to the elementary school in the small town of Klawock, which is named for the sound the raven makes.

With the children's education taken care of, it was time to think about their teeth again. At Ketchikan we had learned that there was no orthodontist living in all of southeast Alaska. One did fly in from Seattle on a regular schedule, but Cindy's only visit there made it clear that we did not have enough money even for her dental work, and Randy and Jena had not yet been examined.

Cindy was very disappointed. Her front teeth stuck out, and she was becoming more and more conscious of them. She was no longer a cute little bucktoothed kid; she was a teenager who would be pretty if we could get those teeth straightened.

In February 1978 I heard there was an orthodontist in Prince Rupert, British Columbia, but when I telephoned I learned that he did not live there but flew in from Victoria. His receptionist suggested I call Dr. Victor Lepp, who had an office in Terrace, ninety-six miles inland by road from Prince Rupert. This was pretty far from home, but we got there, had the examinations and decided that by paying in installments we could afford to have all three children done together. The traveling was the catch; each visit meant sailing one-hundred-and-eighty miles over some of the roughest water in North America, driving ninety-six miles more by car and then covering the same distance on the return trip. Fortunately, Dr. Lepp said we needn't make appointments in advance. Whenever we arrived, he would work us in.

So the dental work was begun. The three younger children signed up with the state of Alaska for correspondence courses beginning September 1, 1978, to compensate for the time they would lose from school while their teeth were being straightened, and we moved the floathouse to Port Refugio on Suemez Island, off the west coast of Prince of Wales Island, which was a little bit closer to Prince Rupert. Margery, my oldest daughter and the only one not needing braces, went to live with a family in Klawock, working for her board and room and riding the bus to high school in Craig, seven miles away. I would visit her at school every week when I went to town in the small boat to send and pick up the children's lessons and other mail and groceries. Sometimes we would take the sailboat, and the whole family would go along; other times I would bring Margery back to the floathouse for a weekend and skiff her directly to school Monday morning. It is fifteen miles by water, so all such arrangements depended on the weather.

We had been following this routine for almost a year,

and the work on the children's teeth was progressing well. The winter trips, however, were always rough and uncertain. On this trip, we had left the sailboat in Prince Rupert while we drove to Terrace, the braces had been adjusted, we had returned to Prince Rupert and put the Volkswagen back in storage, done some shopping and prepared the *Home* for the trip back.

The date was Tuesday, February 13, 1979, the time 4 P.M. We cast off and motored out of the harbor. The trip normally required two or three days, more if we encountered bad weather. This time it took much longer. It would be another two months before we saw our floathouse again.

This is the story of that trip, just as we lived it. The account may not be technically accurate, or properly written, but it is how we experienced it, how we saw it and how we remember it. I have set it all down but, when I describe what the others thought and felt, it is because they told me later what they were thinking and feeling.

I have told only what is important to the story. I do not dwell on the natural beauty of the islands and waters of our beloved southeast Alaska. In the weeks that followed, we saw the other side of the coin. We did not see the azure sky and the sea of jade. The tideland we had known as an abundant provider of food, shelter and warmth served up only cold and wind and snow, hunger and pain. The spruce and hemlock did not whisper to us of beauty and peace, security and plenty. They sighed, they moaned, they made what our weakened bodies and failing minds thought were the long-listened-for sounds of approaching rescue. And they lied.

# 1

## THE
## STORM

"WHY do we have to leave so late in the day, Daddy? Why can't we stay in town another night?"

Port Refugio, where we had tied the floathouse, is so isolated—with no one else living there when we are not there—that it was always a treat to visit Prince Rupert, with its shopping malls, heated indoor swimming pool, movie theaters, supermarkets and twenty thousand friendly people. The children hated to leave, especially Jena.

"We don't have any more town money, for one thing, and for another, the weather is right. There's nothing big in the forecast from either the B.C. report or the U.S. one from Annette Island. If Dixon Entrance doesn't look good, we'll anchor up for the night in one of our usual

places in the west side of Melville Island. We should be
out there by dark. Don't complain. You've been in town
for four days now, and seen a movie besides. Be thankful
for what you got; it's longer than we usually stay."

"Did you check out with customs?" That was Randy.

"No. I forgot to check in with them when we got here,
so to check out now would only complicate things."

I knew that the letter of the law had been violated,
but we were conforming to its intent. After all, we had
been making these trips to the orthodontist about every
six weeks during the past year. The customs checks had
become routine, both for them and for us—so much so
that this time, when we arrived at midnight, we just
climbed in our bunks and went to sleep. The customs
office would not be open at that hour anyway. Then, with
all the excitement of waking up the next morning near
town, and having so many things to attend to and shopping to do, I had completely forgotten to call. Next time,
I told myself, I would be sure to remember, but to check
out now would only complicate things for the customs
people as well as ourselves.

Back aboard the boat, while we were still in compara-
tively sheltered waters, we busied ourselves with prepa-
rations for the trip home. The food and other purchases
from Prince Rupert and Terrace were stowed and lashed
down. There was a lot of food aboard; we seldom had the
opportunity to get such things as fresh fruits and vegetables, bakery-made pastries, nuts and fresh meats. We
had also bought a large supply of canned goods.

I made hamburgers and passed them around. Cindy
was at the tiller, with Randy in the pilothouse with her,
to be sure she steered a safe course through the channel
north of Digby Island. Jena, as usual, was in her bunk
with a book. The children asked for the cinnamon rolls
we had bought, but I said we would keep them for a

treat on Valentine's Day, after we were past Dixon Entrance. We could not know that this was the nearest thing to a meal we would have for weeks.

Randy was my first mate. At fifteen he had some growing yet to do, but he was wiry—strong and tireless. He looked like just another skinny little kid, but he was a surprisingly fast runner and an excellent swimmer. I relied on his judgment as well as on his physical strength and agility. He was cautious when caution was called for but did not hesitate to take chances when action was necessary. When the weather was extra bad, the seas especially rough or the course exacting, I would put Randy at the tiller, whether it was his shift or not, and let the others take longer turns when the going was easier. Randy could steer for long periods of time on even the darkest nights, maintaining his course just from the feel of boat and water. The *Home* always seemed to respond favorably to his sure touch. I could sleep with Randy on duty.

Cindy is the dreamer of the family. Sixteen years old, she was small and pretty, with a gleam in her big blue eyes. Though she was casual about it, Cindy had intuitive powers. If she didn't know the answer to some philosophical problem from experience or logic, she would discover it intuitively. Yet few of the problems that so befuddle others ever touched Cindy. She needed only to smile, and the world was hers. Everyone loved Cindy because Cindy loved everyone. But at the helm, her course was apt to wander as easily as her thoughts. I had to keep a sharp lookout when she was in the pilothouse. A safe journey and a sure arrival require more than a loving heart and compassionate nature.

Jena Lynn, my Leo child, was the youngest, and at twelve the most nearsighted of us all. She is badly misplaced in the family order. With the personality and drive of a born leader, she was cast in the role of little sister, where her efforts to lead the other children were constantly frustrated. Understandably, she retreated to a private world of literature. Jena did not just read books that were on hand—she would seek out entire libraries. Ironically, one of her favorites was *Cradle of the Deep* * by Joan Lowell, the autobiography of a young woman who, from the time she was a year old until she was seventeen, lived aboard her father's sailing ship. The ship sank off the coast of Tasmania and she and her father swam to safety.

At the tiller Jena was exacting, but forceful and demanding, never learning the "feel" needed to make the sailboat respond easily to her wishes. Her strength of character was to serve her well in the struggle that lay ahead, a struggle few could have survived, whatever their physical strength and endurance—and Jena weighed only a hundred pounds.

I had checked the radio weather forecasts before leaving the harbor in Prince Rupert. The report from British Columbia told of a storm system to the west of the Queen Charlotte Islands. These storms should move south and east. We had winds of ten to fifteen knots from the southeast, which made good sailing conditions for us. As we entered Chatham Sound we had unlimited visibility. We put up the genoa jib, our largest, and were making good time on a broad reach, with the wind on port beam. slowly shifting to port quarter as we neared Brown Passage.

Visibility was good as we entered Brown Passage, with Melville Island on the north and Stephens Island to the south. It was starting to get dark, but the moon was just

* Lowell, Joan, *Cradle of the Deep* (New York: Simon and Schuster, 1929).

past full and from behind scattered clouds it gave good light. We could see a snow squall with a white front in Hecate Strait south of us. It was nearly stationary, or at least it was moving slower than we were. No storms were visible to the north and west, the direction we would travel as we angled across Dixon Entrance to the west side of Prince of Wales Island.

By the time we left Triple Island Light and the west end of Brown Passage behind us, it had gotten dark, but conditions still looked good for the passage. The wind was now on our stern, and our jib was pulling well. I had left the engine running too. The temperature was near the freezing mark so the heater that ran from the engine was welcome; also, the extra speed would get us across that much sooner. The U.S. weather report, from Annette Island to the north, had spoken only of east wind for Dixon Entrance. That would be the wind that blows from Portland Canal. Fine, I thought. When we get far enough out for it to affect us, it will be just a breeze, and on our tail besides.

So we were committed to our course. It would be a long night, but by morning we should have the worst part of our trip home behind us.

The sail plan of the *Home* was originally designed as a conventional ketch with an open cockpit. Motoring about in the wet, cold, windy climate of British Columbia that first winter had showed us the importance of an enclosed pilothouse, so I designed and built one. The sail plan then had to be altered to fit it. The result was a simple, inexpensive, functional sailing arrangement that served our needs well, being safer for my young crew to sail than the standard rigging. We sailed with two loose-footed jibs; no booms or gaffs to endanger anyone on deck.

The three children normally arranged the time at the

tiller themselves. I would alter their shifts only in special circumstances. As the night progressed they were rotating, each staying one hour on the tiller and then having two hours off. I seldom steered the boat because the constant movement of rudder and tiller tended to aggravate my rheumatic condition. I did the things that required less physical exertion—cooking, tending the engine and just being in the pilothouse when the children needed advice or moral support. I always tried to go up to the pilothouse several times each hour when Cindy or Jena was on duty, to see how the sails were drawing; to check the speed of the boat, our position, the compass heading and the weather; and to talk with either girl for a while. This was especially good for them at night. When Randy took over for his stint, I knew the boat was in capable hands and I would try to get some sleep.

As I lay in my bunk that night I noticed the increasing motion of the boat but attributed it to our lengthening distance from Brown Passage. As we advanced farther into Dixon Entrance the tail wind would have traveled a longer distance over open water and created larger swells.

Then I was jolted back to our present situation by Jena's shout down the hatchway: "Randy, will you come up and take over? I can't hold course."

Randy was grumbling as he prepared to go topside. His shift was over and he had hoped for some rest, but because of his recent stint up there he knew what she was talking about. He was needed, so he would go. We went up together. The wind definitely had increased, and light powdery snow was starting to pile up in the corners of the pilothouse windows. The one headsail we had up was putting too much strain on the rigging. The seas were getting big enough to make the boat surf out of control as it crested them.

Randy took the tiller and suggested that we lower sail

and put up no more than storm headsail. But with the dark, the snow, the increasing wind veolcity, the size of the seas and only the children for crew (capable though they were), I had to say no.

"If we had winches, I would reef in and spill most of the wind from the sail. As it is, we'll just let some sheet line out so the sail we have up can't present such a large surface to the wind." The result may have looked like anything but proper sailing, but it served the purpose and there certainly was no one to see it.

"What do you figure as our position?" Randy asked. "It's snowing heavier all the time. It's increased just since I went below a few minutes ago."

"We've been making terrific time with this tail wind," I said. "We're probably just a few miles south of Celestial Reef. That would account for the increased wind. We're out of the lee of Dundas and Zayas islands and getting the full force of the Portland Canal winds. I didn't expect them to be so strong this far out, and the weather report said nothing about snow with them. If visibility improves we should be able to see Cape Chacon Light within an hour. Hang in there a while longer, and let's see how things are then."

I went below to my bunk feeling nauseated. Had I eaten something that made me sick? If I stayed up there any longer, I would have heaved, and then Randy would have teased me about being seasick. I was a Marine in the Pacific during World War II while still a teenager, spending as much as a month at a time aboard ship. When the Korean War started, I signed up with the Military Sea Transport Service and lived aboard ship for almost two years while helping move troops across the Pacific. Then I had spent six years fishing commercially in Alaska's Cook Inlet. We had been sailing the *Home* for almost five years, living aboard much of the time. In all this time and under such varying conditions, I had never been seasick. What the hell was going on now?

About that time, I had no control over it, whatever it was. I just made it topside and got my head out of the pilothouse in time. So much for the hamburgers. They must have been spoiled. I'd keep a close watch on the children to see if they were affected. I emptied my stomach and returned to my bunk.

"Dad, this isn't letting up at all. In fact it's snowing harder. I can't see anything." Randy sounded very concerned.

"All right, I'll be right up." God, I'm sick, I thought. I hope I don't puke in the cabin. I had to get up there, though.

As I put my head up through the hatch, I was startled to see only snow—and it was horizontal. Visibility was down to less than a hundred yards. Big breaking waves were coming out of that white wall behind us, their tops foaming. They would be almost on us before they were visible. Randy was trying hard to hold course, but the boat seemed to have a mind of its own.

"We'll have to go to sea anchor, Randy." This is not a hook that grabs bottom; the water was much too deep and the seas too violent for that. It is a device that offers resistance as a bucket does, when you try to pull it through the water quickly. Tied to the bow, it holds the boat head on to the wind and slows its drift. We had never had an occasion to use a sea anchor before, and not being affluent enough to have everything aboard that we might someday need, a real sea anchor was among the missing.

"Get up here, you girls. We have work to do."

When they got to the pilothouse, I told them what I had in mind. We couldn't risk continuing across Dixon Entrance in this weather. We would be on the rocks in heavy surf before we knew it. So to slow our forward movement, we would drop the headsail and use it as a drogue. With one corner lashed to the bowsprit, we would sheet the two remaining corners to opposite rails of the boat. In the water it would form a bag and slow our drift. With wind, snow and mountainous seas, the work was slow and dangerous, but we got it done without mishap. With the sail in the water and the power off, the bow of the boat swung around to face the storm.

When I shut off the engine, the storm sounded even more violent than before. The drogue did not hold the bow perfectly into the wind—it wandered around a bit—but I was too sick to do anything more.

"This weather should clear up by daylight. Then we'll be able to see the headlands and determine our position for sure and go on across," I told them.

We went to our bunks and arranged our bedding to restrict the motion of our bodies as the boat pitched and rolled. It was midnight. I took a bucket with me as I went below, more for propriety than utility, as my stomach by now was completely empty. Regardless of how much retching and heaving I did, all I could bring up were a few foul-tasting drops.

## FEBRUARY 14

Daylight on St. Valentine's Day brought no improvement in the weather. Hard-driven snow continued to block the view beyond a hundred-yard circle surrounding the boat, and the wind held to a steady scream, turning the sea to a frothing range of ragged peaks that bucked and twisted the boat constantly. The drogue held the bow poorly into the wind, allowing the hull to slip sideways between the huge troughs, where the waves could batter us from the side with full force. To move from the pilothouse to the open deck was slow and hazardous, even if one did nothing except hold on, but we managed to put the carpet from the cabin floor out on a line. It stayed on top of the water like a sled, however, so we pulled it back in and tied it to our danforth anchor, a light folding anchor. We put them out together to force the carpet underwater. It seemed slightly more effective that way.

Randy suggested putting up a riding sail, which would sheet tight in a fore-and-aft position between the two masts. I didn't dare try it, even though I knew that it would help restrict the rolling of the hull as well as help to hold the bow to the wind. "It's too dangerous to be handling sail in this wind," I said. "It could so easily flip one of us overboard—and then there would be nothing the others could do. That person would be gone forever."

Several times during the day, the battering was so strong that Randy and I hurried to the pilothouse, sure that we had struck a reef, but we never saw anything, and our checks of the depth sounder revealed no bottom, so we knew we were in water over six hundred feet deep.

Motion sickness had left us all weak and exhausted. I was obviously most affected. Jena heaved occasionally, and Randy and Cindy just felt rotten. I checked the compass heading and the wind direction every half hour. The bilge pump was electric, operated by pressing a switch on the engine control panel, near my bunk. About once each hour I activated the pump until I heard the sound of air sucking into the intake. I spent the rest of the time in my bunk, suffering agonies I had never experienced before. If I have suddenly become vulnerable to seasickness as debilitating as this, I thought, I will move to Kansas.

I thought we must have come within ten or fifteen miles of Cape Chacon on Prince of Wales Island the night before, and since we were moving in a westerly direction, we should be able to see land if the weather cleared at all. If we drifted past Cape Chacon, we would come within view of Long Island; if we passed that, there was still Cape Muzon, jutting out into Dixon Entrance at the end of Dall Island. I watched for even the slightest break in the weather that would allow us to head for shelter.

Randy made an occasional trip to the pilothouse with me, and a few trips on his own, but mostly the children spent the time lying in their bunks. Their nausea and the constant motion kept them from doing much else. Except for practical boat matters, even talking seemed artificial. Hours passed when no one spoke a word.

In addition to the staple foods we had purchased in Prince Rupert, we had splurged on one item, those fresh cinnamon rolls the children had asked for. They were covered with sticky icing, so I had placed them in a plastic cake pan to stow them easier and guard against casual raiding before Valentine's Day. Now no one was interested in the rolls, or in any of the rest of the food we carried.

Either Randy or Cindy was usually seated on the fourth step leading from the cabin to the pilothouse, holding on tightly. From this favorite position, one's head was even with the small windows that were above deck level, and the outside world was then within view. One or the other watched as a gigantic swell would race out of the snowy wall, strike us a loud jarring blow and continue on, thundering and hissing out of sight.

Jena was used to spending time in her bunk reading. She often went through two paperbacks during a trip to and from Prince Rupert. And in the past, when the seas grew rough, she was always more than willing to retire to her sleeping bag—as the others performed the deck chores. But today her uneasiness over the storm and the dizziness caused by focusing on a page kept her from her book.

When the storm began to rudely empty the shelves, we moved the heavier boxes of canned goods to the center aisle in the cabin to prevent them from being thrown down. This left the passageway packed tight with boxes, packages, clothing and odd items that refused to stay shelved. We had purchased, on sale, two large plastic bags of shelled peanuts when we had been in Terrace. Thrown to the floor, the bags had burst open on impact and scattered across the already confused scene. Even though we moved about very little in the cabin, every step crushed more peanuts into the wet floor.

"When we do get home, we'll have plenty of peanut butter," Randy said.

No one laughed at his weak joke, but the thought of home helped relieve our anxiety. While we were riding the storm fairly well, the uncertainties continued to weigh on us. Our location was pure conjecture, based on probabilities of wind speed, wind direction, our rate of drift and tidal currents. I guessed at midday that we were somewhere near the mouth of Dixon Entrance, between Cape Muzon to the north and Langara Island to the south. If my calculations were correct, we would be way out into the Pacific Ocean by nightfall, with the possibility of being pushed farther should these conditions continue.

The storm had been a freak one, coming from the east off the land. The southeasterly storms we were used to lasted up to three days, but we had no way of knowing how long this one would take to blow itself out.

From time to time one strange noise or another would break through our numbness to demand explanation or attention, causing me to venture on deck to tighten a snapping halyard or perform some other minor maintenance chore. I was always surprised to find the decks, cabin top, even the pilothouse free of snow. We must have been taking enough solid water completely over us to keep it washed clear. Late in the afternoon, above the roar of the storm, a loud bang, like a rifle shot, startled us. Going on deck, I discovered that a five-eighths-inch bolt securing the rear mast stay had sheared from the strain. I fastened it as best as I could to one of the shrouds to stop its wild, destructive whipping. When I returned below, everyone wanted to know what it was. "Was it the mast?" Cindy asked.

"No, it's nothing to worry about," I said, trying to play down the damage. The others were quiet.

Cindy broke the silence. "Daddy, if we had a CB, could we reach anyone now?"

"No, darlin'," I replied slowly. "We're over a hundred miles from Rupert. Nobody would hear us unless they were out here too. Besides, no one in their right mind would try to find us in this storm anyway. We'll make it."

We had a radio direction finder, but to use an RDF would require a stable surface, one far steadier than our constantly rolling, bucking boat could provide. My condition—I still was very sick to my stomach—also would have made its use difficult and unsure. We used it mainly as an AM receiver. In the storm we didn't even do that. Radar is what we really needed, but radar had always been financially out of reach.

The *Home* was taking a brutal beating from the cold bullying sea, while being held by wind and blindfolded by snow. Damage so far had been minor and superficial, but she couldn't take it forever. We could sympathize with her in her agony. We shared it.

Toward evening, the winds were unchanged, but the seas grew steadily more violent. The waves peaked sharper and more unevenly, pitching the bow off the wind and exposing us broadside to the powerful, breaking crests of the swells. We had been pounded from the side all day, but now the seas became really destructive.

The first resounding impact turned the hull on its side, hurling people and cargo into the air and slamming us against the opposite wall. I was thrown from my bunk across the cabin onto the galley counter and crammed into the space above the countertop. My forehead struck a sharp edge, opening a gash above my left eye that bled freely down the side of my face and neck. Jena flew eight feet from her upper bunk into Cindy's, striking her knee-cap painfully in the process. Randy found himself pressed against the shelves opposite his bunk. Cindy, already against the far wall, was rolled up the side of the hull and pinned there momentarily until the boat righted itself again.

The cabin was in total bedlam. Jena cried in pain, rubbing her knee. Cindy looked to me for some consolation, an assurance that the worst was over, but I could only pick myself up from the counter as another wall of water broadsided us.

We braced ourselves as the combing swells caught the exposed side again and again, driving the hull over, burying the deck under tons of water and sending torrents down the hatch. The children watched the cabin windows, certain they would shatter inward.

An instant later, over the pounding sounds of wind and water, we heard the splintering and tearing of wood, as if the superstructure was being smashed or torn away. Looking out the cabin windows, the children saw the broken doors from the pilothouse on the top of a nearby swell.

As the last crashing wave spun the hull around, the violence tempered to its original pattern, with the bow quartering the oncoming swells. Randy and I investigated the damage to the pilothouse soon afterward and confirmed the loss of the doors; worse, we found the tiller arm snapped off at the rudder yoke and lying loose in the cockpit amid a sifting of snow already drifting through the openings where the doors had been. The doors could be replaced at a later time. The broken tiller, however, was a different matter and would need repair before the boat could move efficiently under sail or power. I thought I could fix it temporarily as soon as the weather quieted down a little. Until then the seas were far too rough to be back there working on it. I sure didn't feel like doing it—and we didn't need it yet anyway.

What little light the dark skies had given during the day was now gone. I looked around again. Even in the darkness I could still see about as far as during the day. I had been so sure it would clear enough for us to see our position by evening and find our way to one of the secure anchorages we knew so well, but I realized now we would have to spend at least another night just hanging in there.

I went below for the last time that day, found a half-dry sleeping bag, and laid it out on my wet foam pad. My stomach had been emptied many times over and now burned from an accumulation of acid. I knew that I had to stay sharp and be able to do what would become necessary, but I felt awfully weak and sick and had to force my mind to function.

I told the children it would all be over in the morning and we could set sail for home. When they asked me about keeping a watch, I said, "We're out in the open Pacific, and as near as I can figure there are no reefs or headlands—nothing we could hit. There might be a few coastwise ships out here, but they'll pick us up on radar and steer clear." I told them to stay in their bunks and try to get some rest before morning.

Remembering the violent rolls earlier in the evening, I braced myself more firmly in my bunk. Jena joined Cindy in a lee-side bunk that sloped away from the aisle and avoided the more frequent dripping of the windward windows. When we had built the boat, the plans called only for several small portholes spaced along the upper cabin. I suspected that the boat might serve as our home for quite some time and couldn't imagine my children having to live in some half-lit cave, so I had altered the plans by placing five narrow sliding windows end to end on each side along the full length of the cabin. The result provided much more light, but unfortunately the sliding feature had, in the past, allowed an occasional big wave, especially from the stern, to squeeze its way past the overlap of the glass and to drip into the bunk area. This storm confirmed the seaworthiness of the original portholes. These waves carried such a volume of water and washed over the railing with such force that the water literally squirted through the overlap and onto the girls' bedding. Even fully dressed, inside their sleeping bags, with a patchwork quilt spread over them, they were too cold to be comfortable. I had run the auxiliary engine a few times during the day to keep the batteries charged and add heat to the cabin, but it had been several hours since that now, and the cabin temperature gradually dropped to freezing.

It was still too rough and windy to build a fire in the tiny ship's stove. With the sails up we were never able to keep a fire going; the wind that spilled off the sails downdrafted onto the smokestack and pushed the smoke back into the cabin. With bare masts, though, it was unusual not to be able to use the stove. But the winds were much too strong, even for the new storm cap I had fitted to the stack after losing the last one to a howling gale. The danger of a rocking stove and the reluctance of anyone to tend the fire also precluded it.

In the crowded space, Cindy curled into a fetal position with her back to Jena, staring out into the snow and darkness through the cabin windows opposite her. She could not sleep. Although her younger sister had stopped vomiting, she still cried occasionally from the pain in her knee. She needed Cindy for comfort.

Randy lay in his usual quarters in the forward compartment where a blanket hung to cover the entry. Ordinarily the blanket reduced the size of the cabin area being heated, but now Randy's area was no colder than the rest. Cindy had tried to convince him to move to a main-cabin bunk where he wouldn't be as subject to the extreme rise and fall of the bow. But either force of habit or his private nature kept him where he was. It was difficult for him to accept his seasickness. In the two summers he had spent as a helper fishing on a seine boat, he had not been sick once. He was used to taking over at the helm when others were tired or otherwise unable. Now, when he thought someone should be in the pilothouse standing watch, his sickness made it impossible for him to be upright for any length of time without becoming violently ill. Even if he had been able to do it, my estimate of our present position made standing watch seem useless. At midday, when I had judged our position to be at the mouth of Dixon Entrance, Randy had accepted it. Since then, the east winds had continued to batter us, so it seemed logical that we were somewhere out in the Pacific, beyond either the threat or the promise of any land mass.

The reasoning had seemed logical to me, but as I lay in my bunk my dulled mind picked at it, trying to find flaws. One of my concerns during the day had been the precise wind direction. It bothered me that my wind checks had revealed a slight northerly edge to the east wind. A true northeast wind could blow us south onto the reefs surrounding Langara Island. With the wind so strong, and figuring a conservative drift of only two miles per hour, we would have reached Langara by two o'clock that afternoon. But the wind had been only slightly to the north of east, and it was now long past two o'clock. Surely, I figured, we had cleared Dixon Entrance long ago. Still, what if we had approached closer to Cape Chacon than I had realized? Wouldn't that put us within reach of the powerful tidal currents into Clarence Strait and Cordova Bay? But the wind and seas were battering us on the port side, which would be exposed to the north. Wouldn't that force us steadily in the opposite direction?

As the hours passed, I rarely got up. I checked the visibility from below. It seemed to have improved slightly, but it was with great difficulty that I traveled the passageway. I noticed Cindy watching me as I moved around unsteadily. I felt very weak, and my stomach muscles would make their violent contractions at times and places of their own choosing.

I started the engine occasionally. It would keep the battery warm and in peak condition, as well as providing some heat for the cabin for a few minutes. I didn't want the engine to get too cold either. If we needed it in a hurry I could not risk having it fail to start immediately.

It had given us some trouble in the past. On an earlier trip to the dentist we had anchored in Minnie Bay, near Cape Chacon, and in the morning the engine had refused to start. We were forced to scull the boat out of the protected bay by pushing the rudder back and forth like a fish tail. Once out of the bay, the southeast winds refused to blow, and I had to disassemble the starter before finding the problem. The engine started easier now but the incident had made a strong impression on us, and in spite of my weakness I continued to keep the engine ready should we need it.

When the hinged flap above the sliding door leading to the pilothouse fell open for the third time that evening, I asked Cindy to fix it. The pitching and rolling of the boat had tipped it forward, letting in the snow and freezing air. She had suffered the least from seasickness and presumably could get up without consequences.

She found our large serving spoon among the scattered utensils that had once been part of the well-ordered galley. This time she proposed to secure the flap so that it would stay. To keep her balance she clung to the bunk first, then transferred to the stair rail and, in a sitting position, moved up the stairs one step at a time, and wedged the spoon between the hatch cover and the flap.

By now we had gone nearly two days without real rest and one day without food. Twenty-four hours of storm had numbed any fear we might have felt, replacing it with exhaustion and anxiety. As we lay tensely in our bunks, we could hear the creaking and groaning of the woodwork being stressed between the sides of the hull. Outside, the storm continued to tear the tops from the twenty-foot swells and to throw the boat easily from trough to trough. We braced ourselves in our bunks and waited.

Cindy remained wide awake, watchful and obviously worried. She was so optimistic by nature, and usually so quick to lapse into sound restful sleep, that this behavior was easily noticeable. She sometimes had premonitions and would accurately foretell things of which the rest of us had no inkling. Of what she now felt, she said nothing until later, but she could not hide its disturbing effect on her.

As she lay in her bunk deep in her unspoken—really unspeakable—feelings, she watched snow, sky, wind and water through the narrow windows higher up in the opposite wall. As the boat rolled and the window through which she was watching descended, she would see first the cloudy sky, made visible by the moon above it, now only three days beyond full. Further descent brought sky and snow, then a mixing with spray from the crests of the wind-whipped swells. When the boat reached the bottom of its decline, only the dark gray of solid water was visible. The scene would be replayed in reverse as the boat rolled in the other direction.

She lay there for hours as this was repeated, watching and waiting. Then, near midnight, a darker object appeared momentarily amid the jumble of sky and water. She waited for the replay so she could focus on it exactly.

"Daddy, there's land! I know it's land!"

# 2

# IN THE WATER

I leaped from my bunk and turned the key to start the engine. Opening the hatch, I was inside the pilothouse and looking into the dimly lit night before my thoughts started to catch up with my body. The stark terror of the scene forced down my nausea and shocked me awake. "My God! We're on the beach!" I yelled. "Randy, get out of there! Pull those lines in!"

Cindy's first view of land had been a distant point farther along the beach, but from the pilothouse I could see the full enormity of where we were. Surf was exploding against cliffs a mere fifty feet away. Above that the forest rose hundreds of feet from the water's edge, blotting out the horizon entirely with only an occasional silvery snag showing against the dark mass of evergreens.

Snow covered the entire scene above the reach of the leaping water. As the boat rocked and slid closer to the breaking edge of the giant swells, the waves grew sharper and tipped the craft more precariously. We were being pushed sideways toward sure destruction by the full force of the storm.

There was no time to pull in the lines to the sea anchors. The next giant swell could smash our little craft against the steep dark cliffs as easily and thoroughly as breaking an eggshell—with the children still below, unprepared.

A quick glance showed that our nearest escape route lay to the south. Only one hundred yards distant, a rocky outcrop ended all view of land, and beyond it only troubled water was visible. Those same open stretches that we had wanted so badly to be free of for the past twenty-four hours appeared as heaven compared to the alternative. So close. Just to be out abreast of those rocks would be enough; wind and wave would then move us beyond and into the lee of the threatening cliffs.

Any brief seconds that the "powers that be" may have allotted for decision making had expired. I put the boat in gear, advanced the throttle to half and stepped from the pilothouse, moving aft. I knelt in the space where the tiller had been and grasped the rudder yoke. By holding steady pressure to it, I forced it to turn slowly in the desired direction. As the heavy hull came slowly to life, its bow began turning to meet the monstrous, breaking swells head on.

Jena had been nearly asleep when Cindy sighted land. The urgency of my commands to Randy finally brought her from her bunk, but at the window, without her glasses, which were lost somewhere on the boat, she could see nothing but whiteness. Cindy kept saying, "It's right there! Don't you see it?" Jena squinted in the direction

Cindy pointed and even braced herself, expecting to hit at any time, but couldn't see the danger itself.

Randy was still in his underwear but had found his glasses. Looking to where his sister pointed, he took only a second before racing back to his bunk to dress. He had removed his wet clothes earlier and had to feel around in the dim light to retrieve them. Of his two pairs of socks, he could find only half of each pair. He heard the engine accelerate.

"Randy, hurry!" Cindy yelled.

We moved slowly away from the certain destruction where violent sea met immovable rock. Halfway now, only fifty yards to go.

Randy struggled into his hip boots and moved quickly toward the hatch, stepping on the bags and boxes scattered in the aisle and pushing off from bunks and cupboards to maintain his balance. He had seen how close we were to the beach, but in spite of that danger, the sound of the engine in gear put a greater fear into him. Once a sea-anchor line caught the propeller, it would kill the engine and we would be utterly helpless. He said afterward that he had wanted to yell, "Turn it off! Turn it off!" But, as he reached the stairs, the engine's groan choked suddenly to silence. Randy looked across the cabin at Cindy. "I knew it. I knew it would happen," he said and disappeared up the hatchway.

The running of the ship had always been a balance between my willingness to push to the limit and Randy's sense of caution. He didn't try to overrule me, but he would certainly make his opinion known. Coming back on our last trip from Prince Rupert, I had raised full sail into brisk winds; with low swells and unlimited daylight visibility, the boat charged ahead like a racing sloop. Randy had become increasingly anxious about the strain on the masts and rigging. Finally, he had told me, "At this rate, we're going to end up in a drift pile somewhere." The prediction haunted him now as he came on deck to see our disabled boat being driven onto the rocks. But it was not the time for blame. As he stepped into the pilot-house, I moved past the door opening, on the deck outside, going toward the bow. "Let's get the other anchor down," I yelled, and Randy obeyed.

A heavy cast-iron dreadnaught anchor hung from the bow through the hawsepipe. We seldom used it, but it had drawn comment from others because of its pretension toward a much larger vessel. It was jammed tight in the hole. I asked Randy to find a crowbar to work it free, but before he could return, I straddled the bow railing and kicked the anchor to knock it loose. As it broke free, rattling its heavy chain, a huge swell engulfed the bow, dunking me under. I hung tight to the rail and moved free as the bow lifted again.

Randy had untied the short line leading to the weighted roll of carpeting, leaving the danforth anchor free. Even with two anchors down, I didn't expect to hold position long in the twenty-foot seas. The only hope was to gain time. The engine had moved us an additional fifty yards from the beach, but the sea had already gained back half of that.

Randy was working furiously to untie the lashings that held our small orange-plastic Sport-Yak punt to the cabin roof in front of the cockpit. "Just cut them," I said, and stepped back to the open door, shouting down the hatchway, "Give me a knife."

Jena handed one up to me and I passed it on to Randy. Together we carried the six-foot raft-shaped craft to the stern and dumped it in the water, tying its line to the rail. The tiny boat served as a tender to ferry two people ashore, but it was not a life raft. We planned to load it with food and gear. Perhaps it would take its cargo ashore where we could find it later.

I hurried below to prepare as best I could to abandon ship. "We're going to lose the boat, so get ready," I announced loudly to Cindy and Jena. "We've got about ten minutes."

Already dressed, they were stuffing food and clothing in plastic garbage bags, tying the ends off tight to keep the contents dry and floating. Both wore jeans, heavy sweaters, floatcoats—Cindy's a bright blue, Jena's a reddish orange. Jena had on two pairs of wool knee socks and pile-lined rubber boots, while Cindy, in her haste, could force only one of her gum-soled street shoes over a sock. The other foot was bare inside her shoe.

Randy gathered up several of the full plastic bags and carried them up to the Sport-Yak, which was already taking on water. Its bow line jerked tight as the giant swells tossed the two boats up at different angles. He pulled the punt closer, tossed the bags into the bottom and glanced at the beach once more. The moon had partially broken through the clouds, revealing features he hadn't seen: jagged black cliffs, pounded by enormous breakers exploding into the snow and trees. Seen against the dark mass of the island, the rocks seemed closer, incredibly large and threatening. He told himself that none of us would ever make it ashore alive.

As the certainty of leaving the ship struck Jena, she became more agitated, asking questions no one could answer. Cindy promised to stay with her in the water, which seemed to calm her momentarily, but her fear that they might be trapped should the hull roll over soon turned to panic. I sent her up to the pilothouse, where she continued to plead with her sister. "Cindy! Cindy! Get up here! Hurry!"

Cindy shut out the panic and picked rapidly but deliberately through the piles of food and supplies in the aisle, while Randy carried the bags to the Sport-Yak. I searched through the rest of the cabin and picked up a chart showing all of Dixon Entrance. Pointing to the northernmost island on the Canadian side, I said, "That's where we must be, Langara."

Cindy and Randy each glanced quickly at it and returned to the task at hand.

On her knees, choosing items of survival while a raging sea drove us to certain disaster, Cindy felt a strange abstraction for an instant. As she told us later, the hours of exhaustion and the bewilderment of having a premonition materialize left her somehow detached from herself. She saw herself, the boat, the others, the cliffs all at once and felt sympathy for our family and marveled at the seriousness of our efforts to survive. Why were we going to such lengths? No one would know we had been wrecked. No one would know where to look. And if, by chance, we did make it ashore, even we wouldn't know where we were . . .

Suddenly, she was back in the present, watching her hand stuff a container of oatmeal into the sack before her. She carried it up the hatch to the punt, but the bow line had already snapped, sending the tiny craft toward shore to be buried under tons of ocean.

We began placing our survival supplies in the pilothouse after Randy made room by throwing overboard a pile of Styrofoam sheets we had been carrying. The children reasoned that the sacks in the pilothouse would be washed free as the boat went down. When I saw that the items I meant to be thrown overboard were still on deck, I understood. After years of training the children to avoid losing anything over the side, they couldn't bring themselves to break the discipline, even now.

We seemed isolated in our own world. Conditions for the past twenty-four hours had made any conversation impossible, except that of the most necessary and urgent nature. The Armageddon of violent forces we now faced could not be approached hand in hand. We would each be dependent on our own individual strengths, judgments and drives, each hampered by our personal weaknesses and inabilities. We would not have the help, comfort and assurance of interdependency that had always served our little group so well in the past.

Communication was largely by questioning glances, gestures and pantomime, the necessary words shouted over the thunder of the nearby surf.

With a questioning look, Randy handed me our .22-caliber rifle with the loaded magazine inserted. I could easily read his thoughts. It could provide food; it could make us heard and so help to effect our rescue. I smiled, shook my head, and tossed it aside. It would restrict the movements of anyone carrying it and in the surf it could become a deadly projectile.

I offered my own questioning glance at the hip boots he was wearing. He countered with a "Don't worry, it's all figured" wink and moved toward his bunk space in the forward compartment to change to footwear that would not be so dangerous in the water.

In the rainy, water-oriented environment of our daily lives Randy wore his hip boots as commonly as a city boy wears sneakers. It would be difficult for him to part with them, but he well knew the heavy, pulling, drowning weight of boots filled with water.

Our limited income had made thrift a studied practice. Nothing was discarded that might have some later utility, however slight or remote. In the jumbled mess that the interior of the boat had become, Randy could find only a pair of outgrown green rubber boots, size five. Though they were too small and too short for him, they had been kept only because they were not completely worn out.

He crammed his rapidly growing, oversized feet, feet only a fifteen-year-old boy can possess, into these boots with difficulty. Our circumstances allowed no time for careful preparation. He would pay dearly for having to wear those too-tight boots.

I wasted the time necessary to glance at each of the three children to be sure that their floatcoats were zipped up too. They were. The coats had been a major cash expenditure requiring much thought and calculation. Only five short months before, we had been facing the approaching winter with all five family members, including Margery, in need of new coats. The flotation devices that I had bought when our boat was first launched were for little kids who no longer existed. They were now grown—or rapidly growing—teenagers. Since we had to update our supply of life jackets, why not spend the money so as to solve both problems with one purchase? A floatcoat looks much like a thigh-length winter jacket but it is lined with one-half inch of closed-cell polyurethane foam in the body, one-quarter inch foam in the sleeves. Though they are a little bulky, these coats are not heavy and are quite warm and fairly water resistant. Four of the five coats thus obtained were soon to have their utility well tested.

Events and circumstances were quickly moving out of our control and we hurried in an effort to keep pace. As the boat returned, stern first, near to the cliffs, a strong tidal current near the shore pulled it parallel to the coastline. It then slowly moved northward as the anchor flukes would catch, hold momentarily, then be lifted loose by the twenty-foot swells. The thunderous release of the sea's energy against solid rock was close beside us. As each incoming comber pushed us broadside toward the rocks, the receding backwash of the earlier one that had been expended against them would move us away, to be battered by the next one coming in.

The ten minutes' time I had estimated was in this way lengthened. The *Home* received a few minutes' reprieve from her death sentence, but the waves she was taking broadside made it a rough, painful struggle.

Several times we were sure the next breaker would dash us to the rocks; then the anchors would catch on the steep, uneven, rocky bottom and the boat would swing to as much as a hundred feet away. Cindy, Randy and I were in the wildly rolling cabin, going through shelves and boxes, trying to think of what we might need and how we could get it ashore. Jena was still in the pilothouse shouting down the hatchway, pleading for us to come up, afraid the boat would go down with us still inside.

First Cindy went up to calm her, then Randy climbed through the hatch. As he entered the pilothouse, either the keel caught on a submerged rock or an especially large wave hit us broadside, or perhaps both simultaneously. The boat rolled a full ninety degrees, and Randy fell through the hole where the pilothouse door had once been and was forced completely underwater. With only black turbulence around him and the pilothouse on top, he fought to free himself. An eternity later, when the boat began righting itself and tons of water streamed from it, Randy had to make a complete turnaround and struggle just as hard to regain the position in the doorway that he had been trying to escape.

Cindy and Jena were tumbled together as the pilothouse was laid on its side and filled with water. There was only black confusion as they grasped for the base of the mizzenmast, doorframes or anything else that would keep them from falling through the door that Randy was trying to escape.

In the cabin, my world rolled into topsy-turvy confusion. I clawed my way toward where I thought the hatch was, only to find the first recognizable object to be my bunk. This, however, told me in which direction to proceed. I found the hatch but was immediately tumbled back and flattened on the cabin floor by the waterfall created as the boat righted and the pilothouse emptied into the cabin.

When I could get to my feet, the water in the cabin was knee deep and rising, and Cindy was shouting down the hatchway for me to get out of there. "The boat's going down, Daddy. Hurry up, we're sinking."

Just before the boat rolled I had been devising a way to get some matches ashore. I had emptied two one-pound jars of seasonings, opened a box of large wooden kitchen matches and put half in each jar, added a candle stub to each, and replaced the lids. Now when I looked around I found the jars floating but sealed, still dry inside, so I grabbed them. As I climbed through the hatch I placed one jar deep down in my clothes and handed the other to Randy, who unzipped his floatcoat, searching for an inner pocket to hold them.

I stepped back down into the cabin, grabbed two foam pads that were floating in the rising water, and took them up to the pilothouse. I knew we couldn't take them ashore with us, but they would float and the wind would do the rest.

Looking back down into the cabin, I saw the outboard gas can that we kept full of diesel oil. In the event of fuel-pump problems, plugged filters or leaks from the main tank, I could connect it directly to the injector pump and have a one-day fuel supply for the small diesel engine. It was floating in the water, moving back and forth as the boat pitched.

As I started through the hatchway to get it, I received a sharp command from Cindy—"Don't do it, Daddy, we're sinking fast"—so I just hung on to the hatchway combing and leaned down. The water inside was deep enough that I caught the gas can on its next trip past and lifted it up through the hatch.

As I looked around, the sky seemed lighter than a half hour ago, when Cindy first sighted land. The clouds must be thinning. The wind was not quite as strong, but the thunder of the surf was just as loud, and it was still snowing lightly.

I heard Randy shout to his sisters, "Stay away from those cliffs and big rocks; they'll kill you. Try for that low spot farther back."

I motioned for the children to move from the pilothouse. The deck was now awash, and the low center section of the rail was also underwater. The breaking crests of the incoming swells drove through the door of the pilothouse and down the hatchway, and the backwash hitting the shore side of the boat was also coming in.

We moved to the stern of the boat and put our feet over the side, sitting on the railing.

"We won't be able to help each other," I told them. "Each one is on their own. Just grab rocks and pull yourselves out when you get to shore. Don't let the water drag you back or you will die.

"Don't stay on the beach in the wind. Go back in the trees, and we will meet there.

"Be ready to go when I tell you . . . Now!" I said as the breaking crest of a swell passed us.

No one moved. Cindy gave me a look that showed the

guilt she felt at not obeying. Her thoughts were obvious. She would go without question, but why did she have to be first?

"Now?" she shouted as the next wave raced by.

"Now!" I repeated.

Cindy slid into the water and pushed herself away from the boat. Jena followed immediately. Cindy let out a loud gasp; the near-freezing water was a shock as it rushed up under their floatcoats.

Randy and I were spared the necessity of making any decision, for the next comber lifted us, but not the boat, and we joined the girls in the dark icy sea.

Jena panicked immediately and started to cry as the cold numbed her body. She grabbed Cindy around the neck from behind and pulled her under the surface. Cindy fought her off and pushed away. I reached out to Jena, trying to calm her, but she immediately wrapped her arms around me. I offered no resistance and spoke as calmly as I could.

"Jena, listen to me. You'll kill us both this way. I can't help you. Nobody can help you. We all have to make it by ourselves." Still sobbing, she released her hold on me and turned to follow Cindy.

As each loudly hissing crest passed us, there would be relative quiet before it broke with booming thunder on the big steep rocks beyond. This gave us a few seconds to speak. I told the kids to move away from the boat and raised a hand above the water to motion them farther astern. I felt sure that as the *Home* settled to the bottom, she would roll on her side. Her tall masts could then deal a fatal blow to anyone they struck.

There was considerable floating debris in the water near us: poles from our rigging, sheets of plywood and Styrofoam we had planned to use for our floathouse, as well as the items that we had thrown overboard or left in the pilothouse to float free.

We instinctively clung to this stuff and watched as the boat continued to settle below the troubled surface. The lights shining through the cabin windows remained clearly visible through the black waters for some time, even after the roof of the pilothouse had slipped from view. Our big twelve-volt storage battery, now completely submerged, was still doing its job as its last life was being drained from it.

Randy asked if it was true that batteries exploded when placed underwater. Our present circumstances prevented technical discussion. I simply replied, "Don't worry about it."

The boat was moving down faster now, as indicated by the masts; still vertical, they were rapidly disappearing. When the tip of the aftermast slipped beneath the surface, the anchor light that usually shone thirty-five feet above the night waters was still glowing, casting a dim artificial light over us nearby.

"How can it do that?" Randy asked.

"I don't know," I replied. And then the *Home* was gone forever.

I knew of the body's tendency to go into shock when subjected to extreme cold. I thought fleetingly of a friend from past years who, when a boat overturned, had been dumped into waters of about this temperature—around 35 degrees Fahrenheit. He wore a life jacket but he was unconscious when pulled out about twenty minutes later, and he died, leaving a wife and five children on a remote Alaskan homestead. The country doctor who examined him soon afterward said that he had not drowned but that the cause of death seemed like surgical shock.

I knew that we must get to the beach and to shelter

quickly if we were to be anything more than four more digits on a list of statistics. I shouted to the children to leave the flotsam they were clinging to and move on. I said that our floatcoats would hold us up and this junk would only hurt us in the surf.

I could easily read Cindy's thoughtful, caring look at me before she turned and began swimming away, closely followed by Jena. My rheumatic problems restricted the use of my arms so that I could not swim strongly but had to rely on a less effective dog paddle. Her look said "good luck" and, if necessary, "goodbye."

As the current caught us, we were strung out into a line of bobbing shapes, rising and falling independently of one another. When we were in the trough of each swell, we were unable to see the beach, but the direction of wind and wave gave us no choice. The swells gradually steepened and snatched up each person separately, surfing us forward, easily at first, then faster as we were caught in the peaking crests. They became waterfalls, hurtling us over the edge and burying us at the bottom of deep trenches, while the ocean hammered and tore at us.

So this is what it's like to die, thought Cindy. Now I will have to take a breath, and I will drown, because it will be water. But as her empty lungs exploded open, her mouth broke through the foam and pulled in half a breath before the next wall thundered down painfully on her head and shoulders, burying her again.

Relax, she told herself. You got through the last one. She let her arms and legs go limp as the turbulence flailed her limbs wildly in all directions. This time, her body rolled and tumbled and popped to the surface sooner. The roaring foam propelled her forward until her knees struck rock; she was on a gradually sloping beach. She tried to stand, but the wave at her back knocked her forward again. A small log, like a pole, danced in the foam beside her. She reached forward and clung to its rough surface. The returning surge swept past her, pulling at her legs until another wave crashed over her, and suddenly she was holding on to a huge rock that rose above the beach. The rock felt solid and ancient, as if it had been there forever. She stood and tried to walk past it, away from the water. The waves no longer struck her, but she stumbled forward each time they crashed behind her, as if their sound still held power.

She moved among the rocks, calling, "Daddy! Randy! Jena!" Suddenly, she saw an orange floatcoat silhouetted against the snow. "Hey, I'm over here," she called, thinking it was Randy. If anyone had made it to the beach, she expected it would be him. He would help her. But as she crawled up the beach, she realized it was Jena, who would be needing her help instead.

Jena leaned against a rock, unable to stand. Except for her socks, she had been stripped naked below the waist by the first wave, losing boots, jeans and even underpants. Fine flecks of snow swirled around her bare legs; the spray, thrown high by the pounding surf, froze to a glaze on the rocks around her. In the freezing wind, she shivered uncontrollably.

Cindy spoke in a flat voice. "We have to get off the beach. Daddy told us to get into the trees, out of the wind . . ." Her voice trailed off, and she collapsed against the rock beside her sister.

After several minutes, Cindy repeated my instructions and stumbled forward as if walking in a dream, leading her sister into the snow. The full moon, covered by only thin clouds, lit up the entire beach. The snow was much deeper than she had thought, coming above her knees, making walking difficult. Next to the beach the trees were thin, scraggly evergreens that offered no protection from the wind. Beyond the beach, the hillside rose nearly straight up. Suddenly Cindy became aware of her sister's nakedness and stared at Jena's bare legs in the snow. "We can't do this. We have to go back," she mumbled aloud, and led the obedient Jena back toward the beach.

The rocks on the beach were free of snow except for caps of white stacked on the taller ones, where the highest tides had advanced and retreated. Cindy searched the dark passages among them for some trace of comfort and shelter. Jena collapsed at the first pause and would not get up. They were in a narrow space between two head-high rocks that blocked most of the wind; the rocks were coated with ice. Brick-sized rubble covered the floor of their chamber and sloped unevenly toward the farthest reach of the surf, several yards away. Cindy wedged in next to Jena, unzipping her floatcoat to cover a portion of Jena's legs. They lay on their backs, with Jena's legs drawn up beside Cindy. They were tense and rigid with cold and unable to sleep.

Several hours passed. The clouds thinned out more, and the wind died to a breeze; the bright moon reflecting on the snow behind them gave the appearance of dawn. Jena spoke. "Cindy, I'm awful hungry." It had now been thirty-six hours since she had eaten her hamburger, and she had lost that to seasickness. Cindy rose stiffly to her feet and peered over the rocks before she realized that it was still night. As she looked toward the water, she recognized several small chunks of Styrofoam that had been washed ashore by the receding waves. Stumbling repeatedly, Cindy made her way through the rocks as Jena watched. None of the bags of food she hoped for were there. She took some Styrofoam back to Jena and placed it under her sister's legs and between her backside and the ice-covered rock wall of their shelter. Then she lay down again and huddled close.

The cresting wave that first grabbed Randy surfed him forward at a frightening speed until he slipped out the back of its leading edge and sank into the deep trough at the face of the next breaker. A wall of water twice his height broke onto him without warning, driving him under and hurtling his body toward the cliffs. But when the spray and foam cleared, Randy suddenly felt rock under him as the retreating surge raked him back. He clawed at the rock and pulled himself to his feet. As he stood crouched in the shallow water, fear urging him on, he discovered he couldn't move his legs. His arms hung like lead; he was totally exhausted by the surf. When another wave crashed behind him, he was pitched forward up the inclined rock. Staggering and falling in the dark, he stumbled into the powdery snow against a nearly vertical slope. He fought the hillside, desperately reaching and pulling, still trying to escape the ocean's pull but unable to move any higher.

Randy later found himself on a ledge thirty feet above the beach; he was lying back against the hillside under a wind-beaten spruce. He couldn't remember how or when he had reached the ledge, but he was satisfied that he was beyond the reach of the surf. Either his fight with the ocean or the extreme cold made his body feel tight, as if all his muscles were contracted. His body shook in spasms. He pulled the hood of his jacket forward and then shoved his hands into its snow-filled pockets. From where he sat, he could see much of the cove below him. He watched the troubled water until daylight.

FEBRUARY 15

At daybreak, Cindy rose numbly to her feet, falling against the rock and holding to it briefly before taking a step. To survive another night, she knew they would need fire, but Randy and I had carried the only matches. Sure that we were dead, she went to search for our bodies.

Although the temperature remained below freezing, the sky had lifted to a ragged gray and the snow had stopped completely. The powerful east wind had fallen to a light breeze that hardly rippled the water between the swells still breaking against the beach. The receding tide exposed a moderately sloping intertidal zone of rubble pried from the cliffs over many thousands of years.

As Cindy stepped from the rocks into the open, she saw another orange coat farther down the beach picking through some wreckage from the boat. It was Randy. She cried out, "Over here!"

Randy looked up, startled, and came over to the rocks. "Just you?" he asked.

"No, Jena too," she answered.

Maybe it was because they could swim faster, or it might have been because they were lighter and floated higher in the water. Whatever the reason, the children had moved rapidly away from me as I progressed toward the rocks.

In the tumbling, spinning confusion of the first breaker, I felt one of my laced-up boots yanked roughly from my foot. I inhaled some salt water but managed to spit and cough it out as the next giant wave dropped, holding me down, spinning, pulling, tearing at me. The other boot was ripped loose, and I was again fighting for air, only to be hammered and rolled again.

Soon I was slammed against a cliff with a nearly vertical face. A large wave lifted me up its steep incline, banging and scraping me along. I clung with hands and bare feet to the icy cracks and sharp barnacles, only to be pulled back by the force of receding water and hammered again.

I thought of my instructions to the children—"You've got to grab those rocks and pull yourselves out! Don't let the water drag you back or you will die!"—and I realized that I couldn't do it myself. I tried several times, but the receding backwash always pulled me loose and dragged me under.

Then I managed to hold for a few seconds and to scramble up a short way before the next swell thundered and leaped up the cliff face for me. It didn't quite reach me, and I climbed higher.

I knew that I should move back into the trees, but the steep rockface above me was vertical, even with some overhang. I was trapped.

As my adrenaline flow slowed, I did too. I was so weak from lack of food and what I later realized was acute illness that the battle with the surf left me totally drained and aching in every joint and muscle. I remember wedging my left knee and arm into a narrow rock crevice so that I would not fall back into the wild water, and then I lost consciousness.

When I again opened my eyes, it was full daylight. I lay a long time just looking around, trying to get things to register. One piece of information would make itself known and then another, but they wouldn't fit together. The tide was out, and the wind had lessened. The surf no longer thundered, and a light sifting of snow lay on the steep rocks beside me and in the folds of my coat.

As my mind slowly began to grasp more of the situation, I thought of the children. I called their names and waited. No answer. I called again. But had I really hollered or did I just imagine it? I couldn't decide, so I tried yet again.

It seemed so odd that I should be alive and they dead. They were stronger swimmers; they had young, supple bodies. At least one of them should have made it ashore and would be still alive nearby.

Or was I even alive? With everything so disjointed and out of focus, I couldn't decide.

Then I noticed my feet, a bloody torn sock on the left one, the right one bare and an unnatural white. From them a tiny trickle of blood ran down a short way to a crimson puddle. It obviously contained gallons. There is not that much blood in the human body. I must be dead.

But my consciousness should be outside of my body looking back at it, not inside it looking out. A pulse would decide for me. I was wearing a pair of wool-lined leather gloves that I had not lost the night before. Removing the right one, I pulled up the left sleeve of my coat to try and find a pulse in my wrist.

I never did feel a heartbeat, but when my hand touched my wrist I felt *myself* and knew that I was alive.

But there was that puddle of blood. Things just did not make sense. I thought of the container of matches and felt for it. It was gone.

I looked up to the snow-covered overhang that had stopped me the night before, then down to the steep rocky beach and my bleeding and frozen feet. No matches, the children gone. I couldn't get to my feet; walking was out of the question. I didn't even know where I was. If I wasn't dead now, I soon would be.

With the end in sight and inevitable, I could see no reason to delay it, or anything wrong with making it sooner. I unzipped my coat and opened the front of it, ex-

posing my wet clothes to the freezing wind. The change
was noticeable and quite uncomfortable. I decided that
just to wait might be easier and zipped up again.

It seems odd that my mind now turned to the Bible. I
have never held it in awe, fear or reverence. It has for
many years been within reach of my bed and consulted
often, but the fundamentalist Christian interpretation I
could not accept. It seemed to speak to me not of the
divinity of one man, on whom my salvation depended,
but rather of the ultimate higher spiritual destiny of all.

But it was to the Bible I now turned in final preparation. I thought of the Sermon on the Mount, the Cruci-
fixion and moved on through Revelation for the beautiful
message it holds for me. I ended with the last verse,
spoken aloud as I remembered it.

"Even so, come quickly, Lord Jesus. Amen."

# 3

## ON THE BEACH

"THERE'S Dad! Right there!" I heard Randy say, but his voice didn't register as part of my world.

Cindy whipped around and looked up directly into the rock crevice where I lay. They had almost passed me by. They had searched far down the beach, but my position deep in the cleft of the rocks hid me until, on their return, they climbed up into the rocks and passed directly below. I heard their voices and saw Cindy's face right in front of me. Then Randy's face popped up over the rocks. I tried to speak, but the words came out broken and difficult to utter.

"I called you. Nobody answered."

"I heard something, but I thought it was the wind," Cindy said. "Are you all right?"

"I've lost a lot of blood. Look at that puddle."

Cindy looked troubled and concerned. She can't lie; her face always reveals her true thoughts. I can read her like a book, and her expression said that I didn't look so good. She glanced at the red pool below my feet.

"That's not all blood, that's saltwater! You'll be okay."

They lifted me out of the crevice, ready to get me up onto my feet. I tried to show them the futility of their efforts.

"I can't walk—they're frozen."

"I'll go get something for his feet," Cindy said and hurried away.

"Have you seen Jena?" I asked Randy after Cindy left.

"Yes, she's just a little way over there where we started a camp. She's all right, but she lost her boots in the surf, and her pants too."

Cindy returned with a bulky green sweater and a boot they had found on the beach. The boot was one of mine, not one I lost in the surf but another from a storage locker on the boat. Cindy carefully pushed the boot onto my left foot and wrapped the bare right foot with the sweater, tying the arms around my ankle. Together they eased me down the steep rock, supporting my shoulders and helping me to the end of the cove close to where Cindy and Jena had spent the night.

In an open gravel area below the snow line, they eased my body to a sitting position. As I saw my youngest daughter, I spoke her name—"Jena"—and lay back, too weak to feel relief, joy or any other emotion. My mind was slow and sluggish. Trying to think was like trying to start a cold engine when the oil is too thick.

Jena hopped on her one booted foot to where I lay and huddled beside me. She seemed shocked and acted as though she wanted to say something, but she only stared at me and shook her head.

Randy gathered some small driftwood for a fire, and as he took out his matches and candle stub, I sat up. Things started to fit together now. There was a better way to start that fire. I was still unable to speak clearly. "Put something on it . . . make it burn. Let me . . . Did you find the gas can?"

Cindy brought forth a small can of white gas. It had been extra fuel for the Coleman lantern on the boat. Randy splashed the fuel onto the damp wood and stood back as my stiff hands fumbled with the matches. I was unable to hold or strike the matches, and Randy finally took them from me. The flames leaped high but burned only a few minutes before flickering out.

"Got to have smaller wood," I said. "Where's the knife?"

"We don't have one, Daddy," said Cindy.

"Why didn't that knife get ashore?"

"I was going to keep it, but you asked for it and I handed it to you," said Jena.

"And I passed it to Randy to cut the Sport-Yak loose with."

"And I gave it right back to you after I used it."

"I tried to return it to Jena Lynn," I said, "but she was in the far end of the cabin so I laid it on the seat in the pilothouse for a moment."

"Then there was that violent roll of the boat, when it and all of us were underwater so long," Cindy said.

So we would have no knife, and only after finding smaller pieces of wood and trying several times with the gasoline could we keep the fire going.

Jena and I huddled close to the flames, Jena turning her bare legs from side to side to warm them. After several minutes of staring blankly at Jena's legs, I reached down and removed the sweater from my foot. "Jena, put this sweater on upside down. Put your legs through the sleeves."

My mind was starting to work better now, the bits and pieces fitting together. Jena's bare legs and butt had caused my memory to reach back twenty years earlier to a Nevada hunting trip.

In early fall, the mountainous high-desert country was quite warm and sunny during the day but near-freezing after the sun went down. My friends and I had parted to hunt separately at 10 A.M., leaving coats and even shirts at our vehicle. By sundown three of us had returned, but one fellow was missing. We started searching immediately. Evening became night; the weather turned cold and clear. Our companion had worn only a light undershirt, but when I found him near midnight he was wearing a bulky sweatshirt. The country we were in was uninhabited, and he had seen no one all day. Where had he gotten the shirt? It turned out he had been wearing the lower half of his long underwear, so when he got cold he took the bottoms off, cut a hole in the crotch for his head and put them on upside down.

Now we could apply that lesson to Jena's problem. Cindy found a short piece of line and tied it around Jena's waist to hold up her improvised jeans, and then she and Randy continued to comb the beach, bringing their finds back to the camp and warming themselves before resuming their search. Cindy found the mate to my leather hunting boot and also the mate to the fashion boot Jena was wearing. At first no one recognized the high-heeled imitation-leather girl's boots, but they had to have come from the wreck, and eventually Cindy remembered that someone had given them to Margery, and she had left them in the boat. None of the boots that Jena and I lost in the surf were found.

Pain began throbbing through my feet as the warmth of the fire penetrated the bare flesh. I said to Cindy, "I can't let my feet thaw. I won't be able to walk at all if they thaw," and started to put on my boots. As I came to the sockless foot, Cindy remembered the wool sock she had put in her pocket before the shipwreck and reached to find it. It was gone. She sat down and took off the one sock she was wearing and gave it to me. I looked at her low-cut street shoes and said, "No, then you don't have any."

"Jena still has two pairs," said Cindy. She reached across, taking two of her sister's knee socks that were drying by the fire. Jena didn't object, now that she had the fashion boots, but she watched carefully as Cindy put the socks on. To Cindy, there was no question; we would share what we had.

As Randy came up to the fire dragging our battered orange Sport-Yak, I told him to stop a minute. "Listen," I said to them, "I'm not thinking real good. If I do or say something that doesn't seem right, stop me, question me —please. I'm just not very sharp yet."

Cindy tried to comfort me and reassure me, but I could see no basis for her optimism. She repeated that I would be all right and that I should not worry. She went away with Randy again to search the beach, leaving Jena and me staring blankly into the fire.

As Cindy and Randy reached the lapping waves, they stood together staring out on the water. Only Randy had managed to save his glasses. Even without hers, Cindy could see there was nothing but open ocean ahead of them. The sun was just a light spot among the gray clouds, but judging from its position they knew they were looking directly south. To the east and west were the dark cliffs that formed their cove. In sharp contrast to the black and jagged cliffs, the tidal zone where they had been searching was a smoothly channeled green shelf of rock stretched one hundred feet from the upper tideline to the abrupt dropoff where they stood. Two hundred feet farther out, Randy could see a marker buoy bobbing on the surface. The other end of its line was tied to the shrimp pot that had been lashed to our boat, now far beneath the surface. He stared at the buoy awhile, showing no emotion.

"Let's go see what's around the point," he said, and began combing the beach to the east. As they cleared the point, they were met by the cold northeast wind and an equally chilling view. Mile after mile of rocky points continued to the northeast. Ten miles offshore in the same direction were several small islands and a faint trace of a larger land mass behind them. It made no sense to Randy. If we were still in Canada, on Langara Island or one of the Queen Charlottes, there should be no small islands to the north or open water to the south.

"Do you know where we are?" Cindy asked.

"I'm not sure, but I think we're on Cape Muzon."

"On Dall Island? How could we have gotten on Dall Island? Daddy said we were on Langara."

"I don't know," he answered, "but it doesn't look right for Langara."

"What's that out there?" asked Cindy, squinting at a mass of drift caught in a large whirlpool offshore.

"There might be some stuff from the boat," Randy replied. "It's mostly a bunch of kelp."

"Somebody could take the Sport-Yak out and check."

"Somebody else could," he said. Although the waves had calmed considerably, Randy's memory of the night before still terrified him.

There was no wreckage from our boat north of the point, and they returned to their cove to continue their search for salvage. Most of the debris was strewn at the high-tide line, but occasionally they found items lodged among the rocks closer to the water. Not knowing what they might be able to use, they brought everything they found to our camp above the reach of the rising tide. There were some things of doubtful value, such as the propane tank from the boat, but there were other items that were highly prized: one of our sails, three foam pads and the six-gallon outboard fuel tank. The tank was heavily dented and gouged but still contained about two gallons of diesel fuel. The white gasoline we used first as a fire starter burned too quickly to catch the wet driftwood; diesel would be much more valuable.

The three foam pads were sheets of open-cell urethane foam we had used as mattresses on our bunks. They were two feet wide by six feet long. Two were one inch thick; the other was two inches thick.

Struggling from the bulky weight, Cindy and Randy half carried, half dragged the wet sail into camp. It was triangular in shape, thirty feet long on both its leading and trailing edges, twenty feet on the bottom. Its coarse synthetic weave was not waterproof, but it was the only shelter material they had found.

The clouds grew heavier as the day progressed, and with the freezing temperatures, more snow seemed to be inevitable. I was still too weak to be of much help, but I directed the children in preparing a shelter. Against the snow line of the beach next to our fire were two large chest-high rocks. I instructed Randy to place two poles atop the rocks and to drape the sail over them, leaving enough sail to cover the back and floor. The opening faced the fire to collect heat, and could also be closed tight if necessary. We wrung out the foam pads and propped them close to the fire to dry.

Besides scavenging wreckage from the beach, Randy and Cindy collected what firewood they could find. A large pile of logs and drift lay in a line along the rear of the cove, but their brittle mantle of snow made it difficult to locate pieces small enough for the fire. What they could find was coated with a crusty ice that hissed and steamed until the outer surface thawed.

The pile of salvage continued to grow. There was a rope ladder, fifty feet of rubber tubing, a pillowcase, a round yellow plastic kitchen container, a comb, one pair of gloves, a girl's vest, our first-aid kit, two oars Randy had bought in Prince Rupert for a larger skiff he had at the floathouse—and a glass Japanese fishing float covered with rope netting.

When Cindy brought the glass float to me, I took it in my hands and stared at it. "How in the world did this get ashore without breaking?"

The float was the size of a basketball. I had found it on Dall Island the year before, and Cindy had hung it in our sailboat for decoration. It was the largest one we had found in all our years of beachcombing, but its sentimental value didn't seem important to us now. We would much rather have had one of the bags of food from the boat.

So far, almost none of the food had turned up. Before locating me, Cindy and Randy had found only six apples and three onions. The onions were undamaged, but the apples had been rolled against the beach so that they were little more than cores. Each of them ate one, and Cindy placed the three others and the onions along the snow bank at the rear of the camp. Jena eyed them and automatically reached for another. Cindy stopped her saying that it might be all the food they would find. She turned out to have been nearly correct. Additional searching turned up only a full plastic container of corn oil and another one almost empty; a nearly empty jar of Tang; a Cheez Whiz jar with a small amount in it; and a small foil packet of seasoning mixture for spaghetti sauce.

We had placed over a month's supply of groceries in plastic bags on deck before the boat went down, and as it became evident that we would find none of it, I exclaimed in disbelief, "There was all that granola and rice and oatmeal. What happened to it?"

"You saw what happened to the apples," Randy answered.

I was not concerned with food for myself; even the thought was repulsive. The children, however, had not eaten in two days. The prospect of a long stay on this snowy winter beach made the lack of food supplies critical.

Later in the afternoon, Randy brought to camp a handful of mussels that he had pulled from the rocks as the tide receded again. We had no knife to open the tightly closed shells, but after he placed them next to the fire, they steamed open, exposing the inner meat. We ordinarily ate clams quite often but had avoided eating this variety of mussels. The hairy black shells with bright orange meat inside had always seemed unappealing when compared to the tasty white butter clams.

Jena and Cindy watched as Randy ate some of the roasted meat.

"Are they any good?" Cindy asked.

"They're okay," he replied. "But they sure don't have much in them for the size of the shell."

Toward evening, I felt stronger and could think more clearly. Bits and pieces of memory, plus what I saw and what the children said, began to fit together into an overall picture. Our pile of salvage was not "everything but the kitchen sink"; instead, the sink was there but little else. It was of light stainless steel but required the attached galley countertop to float it ashore. For the countertop to float free, the entire hull of the boat must have broken open. The turbulence and tidal currents must be just as violent on the bottom as on the surface along this precipitous beach. The boat no longer figured in my thinking, however, except from curiosity. What mattered most was to find something for the kids to eat and a method of traveling. There were so few people anywhere near where we lived that no one would know of our mishap and be looking for us. We had to care for ourselves, and do it quickly.

I could stand and walk now, though my entire body was one big ache—except for my feet, which had no feeling at all. I tilted the sink partially on edge on some coals at the edge of the fire and melted snow in it, then added the meat from some of the mussels and a few pieces from one of the onions. As it simmered, I seasoned it with a small amount of the spaghetti-sauce powder that the children had found. My stomach felt tightly closed to food of any kind, but the one-cup portions of broth were well received by the others—though it had little effect on their hunger. I found that I could drink a small amount of water, if it was warmed to body temperature. The children awarded me the Tang to mix with it, and I felt much indebted to them.

They continued to collect and roast what few mussels they could find. The beach was too exposed to the heavy surf to promote the growth of much marine life, and the solid rock floor didn't allow for clams.

As night came and we sat staring at the fire, I talked to them, not of what we had lost or of the miracle of our reaching the beach alive, but of what lay ahead.

"First, we have to figure out where we are, and then we have to get out of here quickly. I think I'm going to lose some toes, but what I'm afraid of right now is gangrene."

"Randy said he thinks we're on Muzon," Cindy put in.

Randy continued to stir the fire while I looked at him

inquiringly. "I saw some small islands up off that point," he said without looking up. "I don't think we're on Langara."

This was a puzzle. "I don't see how we could have gotten to the north side of the entrance when that wind was pushing us southwest. I'll have to take a look in the morning."

Later in the evening, the wind shifted to the south and large snowflakes began to blow directly into the cove. As the rest of us retreated to the shelter, Randy stayed by the fire, adding wood and staring into the wind-fanned flames. But eventually, as the snow grew heavier, he too came to the shelter of the sail.

Away from the heat of the fire, we shifted positions constantly throughout the night, alternating our exposed surfaces. We slept poorly if at all. The foam inside our flotation jackets cushioned our upper bodies, and we placed a one-inch pad crosswise under our legs. We laid the other two pads on top of us. Several inches of snow collected on the roof of the shelter and dripped continually onto these foam coverings. Even soaked with water, the pads curled upward and allowed what little body heat we had to escape. Randy went out several times during the night to tend the fire. It seemed to us that whenever we looked out, Randy was there, sitting quietly, as if gathering strength from the flames.

FEBRUARY 16

We got up at daylight and built up the dying coals of the fire. It was several minutes before the heat eased the stiffness in our limbs and warmed our wet clothing. The snow had stopped, although the sky continued gray, and the temperatures were well below freezing. I walked down on the beach to try to work some of the stiffness from my legs and body, and also to see if the night tides had delivered any of our food. The aft mast from the boat was in the drift pile at the high-tide line, further evidence of the boat's total destruction. I stood staring at it for a few minutes, wondering how it could be of use. Then I noticed the electrical wire that ran its full length to the mast light at its peak. We might have a use for that. I pulled the wire loose, rolled it up and took it back up to the fire.

As the children ate the three remaining apples, I worked my way toward the point at the eastern limit of the cove. There were our old friends the Barrier Islands, Round Island the closest. Farther on was Minnie Bay, and off in the distance were Bean Island and the southern tip of Prince of Wales. Randy had been right that we were not in Canada. We were in Alaska, but we were near the southern tip of Long Island, not Dall. Randy hadn't recognized the location exactly because he had never seen it from this angle. Since there was very little extension of the island farther south, I guessed we were close to Kaigani Point, at the extreme south end of Long Island. From the rocks to the west we should be able to see Cape Muzon and Dall Island.

Between Dall Island and Long Island lay Kaigani Strait, which led directly into Tlevak Strait and home. Since the eastern or Cordova Bay side of Long Island offered the shortest route to Prince Rupert, we had never traveled this western, or Kaigani side.

Except for the name Kaigani Strait, I could recall only that there was a narrows at its upper end where the water churned and boiled between tides; and about halfway up the strait, on Long Island, was the long-abandoned Indian village of Howkan. There would be no buildings there. It would be about the same distance on either side from where we were to the north end of Long Island. But once we were at the end of Long Island, to the west on Dall Island was Rose Inlet and an occupied cabin. This was the nearest building. Once there, we could hitch a skiff ride and be home in an hour—weather permitting. We knew Rose Inlet. We had explored it in the summer of 1977, and had visited there only a week before, on our way to Prince Rupert. It had begun to get dark as we had come south down Tlevak Strait, and since we would soon have to anchor up for the night anyway, we had gone a few miles out of our way and made a social call on Jim Costales and Sondra Houtary, the young couple living there. Their trapping season was just ending, and they planned to go "outside" in a few days. They told us, however, that their partner, Pat Tolson, would arrive about the time they left.

Since the steep ruggedness of the beach would make it nearly impossible for us to walk, our best hope to get to Rose Inlet was to build a raft. Our usual route was along the Cordova Bay side of Long Island, but that side also lay directly exposed to southeast storms—which a raft could not withstand.

At other times of the year, since the town of Hydaburg was only forty miles away, we might stand a chance of being seen by a passing plane or a boat on the Cordova Bay side. But the fishing season would not begin for another month and the bush planes from Ketchikan used the bay as a detour only when the mountain passes were weathered in. Several times in the past, when we had traveled Cordova Bay in heavy low clouds, we had been startled by planes flying nearly on top of the water, winding their way around Cape Chacon to Ketchikan. But if the visibility was poor enough to force planes to use Cordova Bay, they would probably not see us anyway.

I decided it would be better to rely only on our own

efforts to reach Rose Inlet. The obvious route was on the west side of Long Island, up Kaigani Strait. I guessed it was no farther than twenty-five miles. With just one or two days of southeast winds, we could easily reach the cabin.

I now knew what we had to do and was seized by a sense of urgency. Not only was it necessary to get medical attention for our frozen feet before infection set in, but we also had to get off Kaigani Point and out of our exposed location in order to build the raft. In spite of our condition, my confidence was revived and I hurried back to camp and assembled the children. "We're practically home," I told them. "That's Cordova Bay, and Rose Inlet is right up Kaigani Strait around that point. We have to get off this beach before the next southeaster hits. Bring the Sport-Yak over here, Randy. How bad is it?"

Randy dragged the six-foot plastic skiff into camp. "It's pretty bad. The bottom's all ripped up."

I examined the long splits in the well-worn bottom and the patch still covering an earlier split. The little boat had already lived several lives. When the small bay where we anchored our floathouse near Klawock the winter before had iced over, Randy had used it at low tide as a toboggan to slide down the steep incline of the shore ice and to scoot out across the bay toward the floathouse. The only hazards were the large cracks where the up-lifted ice met the ice of the bay. By staying low and shifting his weight to steer, Randy had managed to avoid the danger in his solo runs. But Jena insisted on joining him, and as the makeshift toboggan hurtled toward an open crack, Randy was unable to control it with his sister aboard. Jena sat upright, attempting to jump clear and the boat had flipped over, dumping them both into open water between the two slabs of ice. Cindy and I watched in horror from the floathouse, less than fifty feet away.

The strong tidal current could easily pull the two of them away from the open lead and under the sheet of ice. After some of the longest seconds I had ever experienced, Randy popped to the surface.

"Get back down there!" I yelled. "Your sister is still underwater!" But as Randy took a deep breath to go under once more, Jena rose sputtering to the surface, and they both climbed out on the ice near the floathouse.

The episode put an end to ice sledding, especially after a small split was discovered in the bottom of the Sport-Yak. The splits now looked much too serious for repair, even if we had had the necessary materials. The Sport-Yak was molded from hard plastic with an outer air chamber and a line threaded through grommets in its perimeter. It was six feet long and perhaps four feet wide. The large tears in the air chamber made it worthless. Placed in the water, the chambers would fill immediately, causing it to ride much too low to support even one person safely.

Now I looked over the pile of salvage for anything that might help us repair the boat. There was nothing in what we had collected, but scattered up and down the beach were small fragments of Styrofoam, none larger than one foot square. They were all that remained from the inch-thick sheets of insulation we had brought with us from Prince Rupert.

"What if we stuffed all that Styrofoam through the cracks?" I asked. "Wouldn't that work?"

We began an assembly line at once, gathering the pieces, breaking them to the proper size and forcing them into the cracks until the air chambers were tightly packed with foam. Although water could still get in, the foam would provide a buoyancy almost equal to the original air space.

"Okay, what have we got here that we want to keep?"
I asked.

"What are we going to do? Where are we going?" Jena
asked, obvious concern showing on her face.

"We're going to build a raft, but we can't do it here.
If we go around the corner a ways, we can get out of the
wind but if we don't hurry up, we're going to be stuck
here." I started rummaging through the pile, setting aside
the rope ladder, the electrical wire and the rubber tubing:
anything that could be used in constructing a raft. "Is
there anything in that first-aid kit, Cindy?"

The small box was nearly empty. There was a roll of
adhesive tape, a container of aspirin, a small half-filled
bottle of Pepto-Bismol, some bandages and a few safety
pins. I had always joked that if we were ever inspected
by the Coast Guard, I would have to claim to be a Christian Scientist because of our sparse medical supplies.
Cindy emptied the contents into the pillowcase. She also
placed the empty plastic container, the packet of seasoning and the comb into her sack. There was nothing
else of any value. I instructed Randy to put the sail, the
pads, the gallon of corn oil and the raft-building materials
into the bottom of the Sport-Yak and to lash them down
securely.

With a short piece of rubber tubing, I siphoned diesel
fuel from the metal tank into the empty corn-oil container
and placed the tank behind a log. I also put the propane
bottle and the net-covered glass float safely above the
tide. Looking at Cindy, I said confidently, "We'll be back
to pick up this stuff later, some nice calm summer day."

I examined what was left of the sheets of plywood from
the boat, but there were no pieces bigger than two feet
square. In the drift pile, however, Randy had found a
piece of plywood that someone else had lost. It was five
feet long and two feet wide, with rounded, well-worn

edges. I thought that it might have some use and placed it over the sail and pads in the bottom of the Sport-Yak. The oars went on the boat last. There were a few items of extra clothing left over: a light jacket, a vest and a pair of girl's dress shoes.

"Does anyone need any of these?" I asked. "Speak up now, because they're not going with us otherwise." No one spoke, and we left them beside the fire. Although the temperature must have been in the low twenties, no one complained of the cold. Our feet and hands were numb, but our upper bodies were tolerable in spite of our wet clothing. The closed-cell foam in the flotation jackets held our body heat much better than its half-inch thickness would have implied. The jackets had kept us afloat and alive in the cold water, cushioned our upper bodies against the rocks in the surf and now protected us from freezing even with wet clothing on.

Our feet gave us the most discomfort, even though each of us now had socks and shoes. The damage had already been done. Randy's size five rubber boots were becoming increasingly uncomfortable. As he sat by the fire during the night his frozen feet had thawed and also swelled, further increasing the constriction. Privately, he was certain the boots were actually making his feet colder by shutting off circulation. But he didn't mention the problem to us.

A cold southeast wind blew directly onshore as Randy and I dragged the loaded Sport-Yak into the water. The surge among the rocks was caused by the heavy swells in the aftermath of the storm, the wind adding only a slight chop.

"You better leave us the matches, Randy. Cindy and I are going to walk the beach. I want you to take the skiff around the point and out of the wind. Put in at the first good spot you find. We'll meet you in a few hours."

"Jena's going with me?" he asked.

"Yes, it'll make it a lot easier having two of you pad-dling, and with her high-heeled boots and no glasses, I don't think she could make it along the rocks anyway." I turned and called to Jena, who was sitting beside the fire.

There was no answer. Jena had feared all morning that she would have to go back out on the water. My call confirmed it, and she broke down and cried, holding tightly to the rock where she was sitting. Cindy went to her and spoke calmly. "You *have* to go. It's the only way we'll get out of here." Cindy took her sister by the arm and led her down the beach. Randy stood in the water, steadying the Sport-Yak as it rose and fell in the surf.

Jena looked out at the heavy swells and sobbed hysteri-cally. "I don't want to go. Please don't make me go."

I took her arm and spoke firmly. "Jena Lynn, get in the boat." I led her into the water and helped her to a kneel-ing position on one side of the plastic punt. While Cindy and I held the small craft steady, Randy climbed in next to her, grabbed an oar and immediately started paddling into the waves.

"Paddle!" he yelled to his sister, who had picked up the other oar.

The surf breaking against the rocks nearly upset them in the first seconds of launching. Jena found her strength in the fear that she would be tossed into the water once more. Still sobbing, she paddled vigorously, trying to match the strong strokes of her brother.

Cindy and I watched tensely as the bright orange boat with the two orange-coated figures broke through the gray walls of water. Each time we lost sight of them among the steep swells, we held our breath until they were tossed high enough to be seen once more. Cindy's stomach churned and gurgled from the tension until she could watch the drama no longer. Her bowels turned to water, and she ran for the logs of the upper beach. By the time she returned, the boat was only a small orange blotch that appeared and disappeared in the rolling swells of Dixon Entrance, moving toward the surf-washed reef at the end of the island.

I had been watching intently, but as they became visible less frequently, I turned away and spoke to Cindy. "Let's make another check of the beach and then get going. We've probably got about a mile of walking ahead of us."

It was about midday before we were satisfied that nothing of any value was being left behind. I had hoped to find some of the food this morning, but as we set out, I was not overly worried that our search had failed to turn up anything new. I expected that we would reach Rose Inlet within two or three days at the latest. In spite of my weakened condition, I was in good spirits. We had a plan, and we were moving to implement it.

The rocky cliff of the cove continued for several hundred yards to a low ragged headland that stood apart from the steep uplift of the island's face. Beyond the headland was a series of reefs and small islands that formed the extreme southern tip of Long Island. Between the headland and the reefs I expected the coastline to be similar to that which we could see ahead of us. But after an hour of struggling along the cliffs between the snowy hillside and the advancing tide, we reached the headland itself and were met by a sight that took the heart from both of us.

"Oh, my God, look at that," I moaned.

Beyond the headland the shore swept inward another half mile before joining the point. Along its nearly vertical face were three deep cuts that led from the ocean's edge even farther into the steep forest of the island.

"We still have to do it," Cindy said and began at once to pick her way through the rocks and into the snow along the top edge of the hundred-foot cliffs. In her hand she carried the pillowcase containing the matches, a comb, two onions, spaghetti seasoning, the contents of the first-aid kit, the nearly empty jar of Tang, the plastic container and the Cheez Whiz jar, also nearly empty. I carried the gallon container of diesel oil. Cindy's feet were already soaked and cold from dodging the waves along the cliffs. As she pushed ahead through the powdery, knee-deep snow, she told me that the pain in her feet had subsided and that they had become numb once again.

I rested several minutes before following my daughter's path through the snow, toward the first of the narrow canyons.

In the Sport-Yak, Randy was driven not by fear but by the task itself as he paddled the miniature craft through the towering swells. From the highest peaks of water, he caught glimpses of land and purposely kept it at a distance. He felt certain the Sport-Yak could take them safely around the point as long as he stayed away from the breaking surf and kept the bow into the waves. Jena tried to keep up the pace, but her arms ached and her heart pounded in her ears. She felt like some mechanism —swinging forward, plunging the oar ahead of her and pulling it back. If she failed to put strength into her pull to counteract Randy's stroke, the boat would immediately swing in her direction and turn broadside to the waves.

Randy urged her ahead with warnings of what would happen should the boat turn at the wrong time. Gradually even these threats failed to work; she gasped hoarsely, "I can't do it"; but as she spoke, the water poured into the boat from the stern and shocked her into renewed effort.

"Just a little farther. Just to those rocks," Randy repeated to her.

But as she raised her eyes toward the goal, it seemed impossibly far, and she collapsed again. Each time she sat back she was pushed ahead by the water sloshing over the stern.

As they came closer to the reefs of the point, Randy searched the surging rocks for a safe passage to keep from having to swing wide around the end. The boiling gaps looked much too dangerous; the only alternative he could see was a half-mile detour farther south. Still paddling forward, he looked back to the north, where the reefs joined Long Island. As a swell lifted them high into the air, he could see water flowing through the narrow channel between the first reef and the island itself. It would be better to capsize there, he thought, than risk continuing farther into the open water. He turned the boat toward the beach. With the seas running behind them, they were pushed quickly into the narrowing channel. Ahead was a surging flow barely wide enough for the Sport-Yak.

"Steer!" he yelled at Jena as they plummeted ahead faster and faster, between rock walls on either side of them. A breaker crested and fell, sending them spinning through the cut and into the quiet water of a shallow cove.

Released from the power of the surf, they let their oars hang freely for several minutes before continuing. Randy realized they were now in Kaigani Strait. Dall Island lay two miles away across the channel to the west. Two hundred yards north was a group of three small islands clinging closely to a gentle gravel point on Long Island. Dozens of snow-covered logs lay end to end along the beach. Sheltered from the strong winds, the spot would be ideal for building a raft.

Randy beached the Sport-Yak on the gentle slope of the gravel inlet just below the reach of overhanging spruce trees. Instead of bare steep rock, an easily sloping forest floor began at the highest reach of the tide. He unlashed the load and arranged the sail on smooth sandy gravel, and he and Jena lay down on several layers of it, pulling the rest over them. From where he lay, Randy could still see the waves surging through the narrow cut at the point. He knew Cindy and I would round the point just above the surge, but he didn't expect us soon. He had been too intent with paddling the punt to look closely at the cliffs, but he had seen enough to be glad that he had not had to approach the cove on foot.

While Jena shivered beside him, Randy kept his eyes on the point. The rising tide eventually forced him, with Jena's help, to move the sail farther up the beach onto the snow. As it began to grow dark, Randy called a long "Hello" up the beach at regular intervals, but after several hours of darkness he gave up and lay back to rest.

As the afternoon wore on, I fell farther and farther behind Cindy. A bed of coals burned constantly in my stomach. Fanned to greater intensity by every movement, my diaphragm would convulse in an effort to rid my stomach of its torment. The retching sound would burst out uncontrollably and at unpredictable times, to be absorbed by the snow and the steep canyon walls.

Cindy waited impatiently, urging me to hurry. The first deep canyon had taken nearly an hour of advancing, retreating and maneuvering until we were forced to follow the cliff edge deeper into the island to where the rocky cut became a snowy ravine. The route was a compromise between the danger of the rock ledge and the dense, snow-choked brush bordering the canyons. The forest became impenetrable between the first and second canyons, and we were forced again to the cliffs. The nearly vertical angle and the pounding of the waves had kept the cliff face almost free of snow. In its jagged roughness, Cindy found a crude natural stairway just out of reach of the waves and followed it to the second canyon. What would have been a path into the canyon and up the far side was now blocked by crashing seas. Rather than backtrack, Cindy picked her way cautiously up fifty feet of sheer rock. I pleaded for rest, but Cindy kept coaxing me on. With the sky already turning dark, we still had two canyons ahead of us.

Inside the second canyon, a giant spruce had fallen, bridging the gap at a steep angle downward. From a distance the bridge looked passable, but as Cindy reached the high end her nerve failed. Over a foot of snow lay atop the slippery surface. It would be necessary to straddle the log and shuffle her way downward. In spite of the time it might save, the risk was too great. She continued deeper into the island, eventually finding a route down into the canyon near the far end. As she reached a near-vertical wall on the opposite side she stopped and waited for me to catch up. Several feet above her reach a large tree root grew out of the snowy incline. The only alternative was to backtrack and try farther up the canyon. "Is there any way we can get up there, Daddy?" I set the jug of diesel in the snow and leaned against the steep wall, interlocking my fingers to form a step for her. I said, "I'm just a tree, Cindy, climb me." She set her pillowcase down and started climbing. When standing on my shoulders, she could easily reach the root. I handed up her bag and the oil. She stuck them into the snow to keep them from falling back, then locked her legs on the tree root and reached down for me.

I will never know how she accomplished that lift. Cindy is certainly no Amazon and I could help her very little, but she pulled me up beside her. From there, though the snow was knee-deep, it was less steep to the top of the ridge beyond.

Slowly, Cindy picked her way to the bottom of the next canyon, checking the footing and making steps in the steep snow-covered surface for me to follow.

I met her there and collapsed in the snow. I pleaded again, "I can't do any more. Please, Cindy. I have to stop."

Near exhaustion herself, Cindy turned to trudge her way down the canyon. "We're almost there. We can't stop now. They're probably just around the point." Then she remembered the small bottle of Pepto-Bismol in her bag and offered it to me. I drank a small amount. The pink liquid soothed my burning stomach but did nothing for my energy, and as I followed her into the gathering darkness, all I could think of was how glad I was that I had sent Jena with Randy.

We were able to traverse the cliffs above the reach of the waves to the mouth of the third canyon, but by now the sky was almost totally dark. Looking down at the waves entering the canyon, it was difficult to judge how far above the water we actually were. We could chance an eight- or ten-foot drop to the water's edge, if we should slip, but any more was too risky. Cindy stopped and waited for me, staring down at something in the water. I moved to her side and followed her gaze.

"Is that a book?" I asked.

"I'm not sure. It could be."

"I'll bet that's our chart book. We need that book. We've got to stop."

"If we go down there, we might not be able to get out. Let's keep going. This is the last canyon. It can't be much farther now."

I thought Cindy was taking the chart book too lightly. We knew where we were, but our lives could depend on some geographical feature of Kaigani Strait that I didn't know. She left me no choice, however, but to follow her into the blackness.

Beyond the third canyon, the cliffs changed to a sharply angled maze of jagged rock, like a field of upturned spears. We could only feel our way in the darkness and were often reduced to crawling, listening to the sound of waves against the nearby shore and sensing the wind for direction. Even in daylight, and on familiar ground, one relies on the feet to feed information to the computer brain concerning irregularities of the surface. With our feet totally numb, and trying to walk in complete darkness (the moon had not yet risen behind the dense clouds), we often had to stoop and feel the rocks with our hands to determine our next step. Sometimes crevices ten feet wide stymied our progress almost totally. When our hands could feel nothing ahead of us, Cindy lowered herself tentatively into the black void, reaching for bottom with outstretched feet. When that failed, we threw snowballs ahead of us, listening for the impact to tell us how wide and deep the gulfs might be. We kept contact with each other by our voices and the sound of our feet scraping on rock. Several times I stretched out my arm to locate Cindy exactly, only to find her standing so close that we were nearly touching.

We could no longer tell how far off we were from the point, and Cindy's assurances that it was only a little way became hollow and weak. Finally, we descended into a deep crevice and were unable to scale the opposite side. I again pleaded with her to stop. "I'm too weak, Cindy.

The dark is spinning all around. Please, we have to stop."

Cindy was exhausted herself and finally relented. We could not stop where we were, however, since the floor of the rocky cut funneled the swells into the crevice and we had no idea whether the tide had peaked or was still rising.

"Let's find a place where we can have a fire first," Cindy said as she moved up the chasm, feeling the sheer black rock with her hands.

Damn, such a stubborn kid, I thought as I was left no choice but to follow her again. When next I bumped into her, she was standing by a large rock with a fissure in the wall behind it. White snow was visible about eight feet above where we stood, with low trees beyond.

"Daddy, you'll have to boost me up, and then I'll pull you up after me."

My unplanned reply was the sound made by the contraction of my stomach muscles. Groaning, I pushed her high enough to reach the top of the barrier, and after much struggling she pulled me up beside her. Rather than crawl down again, we continued up along the top edge of the chasm, helped by the stiff evergreen branches hanging above us. After reaching a possible descent on the far side, we slid a short distance to a wide incline below the ridge. There were no jagged edges or sharp rocky spears. Instead, we found a sand-and-gravel beach under our feet. It seemed a bit lighter now, and the abrupt edge of the snow showed the high-tide line. We could see a few pieces of driftwood. I would go no farther.

Cindy was already gathering wood for a fire. I arranged it and poured some of the diesel on it. As it flamed to life, we used the temporary light to find more wood. We were beside a sheer rock wall, which should shield us from the wind and also reflect the heat from the fire, making us more comfortable. It didn't work out that way. Except for a few rocks, the floor of our bivouac was either snow or trickles of water. There was no place to sit or lie down. The wind, deflected by unseen trees and rocks, was funneled in on us; later on it contained snow. Twice in the night we moved the fire closer to the rock wall, but it was still in the wind and we could feel no reflected heat. We would sit on one end of the larger pieces of wood while the other end burned in the fire. Shifting, moving, turning in an effort to warm all sides, we found that only one side of us would feel the fire while the other side froze. Twice I sat too long in one position and burned places on my floatcoat. While my exterior froze, my stomach was on fire, and though I tried to make it last, the Pepto-Bismol was gone before morning.

Cindy continually reached down to touch the bottoms of her shoes. She could feel no heat through the soles and wanted to keep from burning her feet. Earlier in the day she had felt so much pain it was as if she had burned the bottoms of her feet by thawing them too quickly.

When I told Cindy how thankful I was that Jena had not been with us on the cliffs, she said, "They must have made it . . . but I wonder what they are doing."

"They didn't have any matches."

"That's all right," she said. "I'd gladly trade this fire for the sail."

# 4
# THE
# COVE

THE gray morning light gradually brought a larger circle of objects into focus: the gravel beach, an uprooted tree, a clear path northward. Neither Cindy nor I had slept or could recall even trying to sleep. The night had brought an end to struggle but no rest, only cramped and stiff bodies. Through the light skittering snow, the shores of Dall Island three miles to the west grew more distinct. The beach to the north seemed remarkably flat and gentle compared to the terror of the dark cliffs. We gladly left the smoldering fire, lured onward by the gravel path between the snow and the lapping water.

No more than ten minutes from our camp, Cindy

stopped. A few hundred yards to the north she could see the orange Sport-Yak high on the gravel beach. She was about to speak when she saw the orange coat of her brother.

"There's Randy. They were right there."

"So close," I responded. "I'm not sure I could have made it anyway."

When Randy saw our blue jackets coming from the point, he walked ahead to meet us.

"What happened?" he asked.

"It was those cliffs. They wore me down, and it was just too dark. We had to stop," I answered.

Cindy pointed back to where the beach disappeared around the corner. "We were right there."

"I thought you might go right by us," Randy said. "That's why I put the Sport-Yak up like that. But I was afraid you hadn't seen it in the dark."

"How was it last night?" Cindy asked.

"Cold," he said with a broad smile.

We reached Jena within a few minutes, and I gave orders to move everything fifty yards farther down the beach, out of the wind. From the point where Jena and Randy had camped, the fine brown gravel continued in a crescent shape for another hundred and fifty yards. Beyond this small cove, the shoreline roughened again into low dark cliffs and rocky shelves where thick evergreens overhung the icy water. There would be no chance of continuing on foot.

Our new camp was situated behind the point, at the furthest inward curve of the beach. In front, three small islets clustered around the crescent of gravel. We gathered wood and built a fire against a log at the edge of the snow. The abrupt edge of the eighteen-inch snowbank turned us as effectively as if it had been a high chain-link fence. With our frozen feet and weakened condition

we seldom challenged it but took the way of least resistance, which was the bare beach. At my direction,
Cindy and Randy found several small poles to hold the
sail as a shelter facing the fire. Tired and weak, Cindy
lay down under the sail and went to sleep immediately.
The other two children sat near the fire, leaning against
the logs. Soon I was also asleep.

We had no preconceived plan for the raft. Its design
would depend on what we could find. Strewn along the
tide line lay dozens of logs ranging from small poles to
two- and three-foot-thick giants. We would be able to use
only those that we could move into the water ourselves as
the tides now were not nearly as high as those that had
lifted the logs up there in the first place. Some logs were
as long as fifty feet, many were partially sunk into the
gravel and almost all were under the snow. It would only
be necessary to move the logs a few feet and let the tide
do the rest, but it was still too much. Besides the thousands of pounds of weight, the logs were held tight in
the icy grip of the gravel.

As the tide fell to low water at midday, it exposed a
large gravel flat between the arms of our cove. It was the
third day since the shipwreck and the fourth day since
any of us had eaten anything much except the apples
and a few mussels. Using a stick to dig at the newly
exposed gravel, Randy found several large butter clams.
When he brought them to camp for roasting, Cindy and
I were awake. Cindy and Jena's faces lit up at once. Soon
they too were digging in the flats. The jar containing the
small amount of Cheez Whiz had broken when Cindy's
sack bumped against a rock during our night travels. The
children picked the glass out of what remained and
dipped the hot clam meat in it.

As Randy prepared his clams, he mentioned the diffi-
culties we would have in moving the logs.

"We've got to have either cedar or spruce," I told him. "They'll float the highest."

"I don't think we'll be able to be that choosy," Randy cautioned.

"If we all get together to push on one," I said confidently, "it'll move. We might not have enough rope, though. Have you found anything like that?"

"Not yet," Randy answered, chewing on the tough meat of the roasted clam. "Do you want one of these?"

"As a matter of fact, I was just going to move upwind so I didn't have to smell them."

The children were still hungry when the clams were gone, but they did not want to expend the energy necessary to dig for more. As a person is forced to endure days of cold and lack of food, the natural tendency is to restrict movement, sit or lie still, and turn inward. Hands fumble and drop the things they try to hold, feet become heavy and stumble, body movements must be consciously planned. Ideas don't tumble out for evaluation but must be forced from the deeper recesses of a slow-working mind. These things require the expenditure of energies that are in short supply.

The snow came and went throughout the day, with the gray sky alternately rising to open the view across the strait to Dall Island and then lowering again. I noted with disappointment that the wind which had been gusting from the south had shifted to the north, blowing directly down from Kaigani Strait. Southeast storms are as much a part of this country as the tides and the dense forest. There had been no warm southeast storms for two weeks. Surely the weather would change in our favor soon. I was concerned that the children would lose body heat and not have enough food to replace it. I told them to always keep the hoods up on their floatcoats—a lot

of heat is lost if the head is not covered—and to use the
now-empty Tang jar to warm the water they drank from
a nearby stream.

I left the fire and walked back along the beach. Early
that morning we had seen a large, square, heavy plywood sheet. Returning to it, I flipped it over; it was part
of the rear wall of our pilothouse. The hand rails were
still intact along both outside edges, but the glass was
gone from the small window in its center. It was about
four feet square and should be of some use on the raft.
My feet were hurting now and I asked Cindy and Randy,
who had followed me, to carry the plywood to the camp,
while I trudged along behind. The two older children had
ranged as far as they could, both north and south from
the camp, and had found only a few small scraps of rope
and a large mass of tangled fishnet.

As we moved back toward camp, they told me of a
discussion they had had earlier. They were concerned
about my weakening condition and thought we might
not have time to build a raft and use it. Randy wanted to
take the Sport-Yak and go for help. Cindy wanted to go
with him so that they could travel faster. Before they
left, they could gather a large pile of firewood, and Jena
could keep the fire burning.

"You can't eat even what little we have," Randy said.
"We're going to have to do something quick."

I didn't answer, not knowing whether the children
were right or wrong. Randy was the planner, the steady
one, and in the past I'd sometimes regretted not taking his
advice. But the idea of letting Cindy and him go off in
that little plastic bathtub, while I stayed here in relative
safety—well, it seemed all wrong. They couldn't paddle
the punt against the north wind blowing down Kaigani
Strait, and it was a long way to Rose Inlet. The decision

about what to do would have to wait until conditions were more favorable.

On the way back to camp, I saw a small log that might be movable and stopped to work at it. Cindy and Randy dropped the plywood to help. Each of them found a stick and began levering the log toward the water. Once the ice let loose, the twenty-foot log rolled down the gentle incline. It was to be the only easy log we found. By late afternoon we had managed to roll two more logs to the tideline, but only one was dry enough to float above the water. Wearily, we returned to camp to find Jena still sitting beside the fire.

I was impatient with her. "Jena, get up and do something. Go find some wood or some rope. You can't just sit there."

Without her glasses, Jena's world was only a blur. Her defense was to simplify the situation by limiting it to a seat by the fire or a place under the sail. But as much as she disliked leaving the fire, being singled out for criticism was worse. She wandered aimlessly down the beach a short distance, returned with a few pieces of wood and sat down by the fire once more. "I get too cold away from the fire," she said. The sweater covered most of her upper legs when it was in place, but slipped down at the waist unless she held it. With the neck hole hanging open, cold drafts blew directly onto her bare thighs as she moved about.

"We've got to do something else with Jena's sweater, Cindy. Can't you keep it up at the waist and tie that hole off so she can move around better?"

Cindy worked at it for a while, but the results still seemed unsatisfactory.

"I can fix that," I said. I walked a few feet from camp

and then sat down and removed my boots and pants. Cindy followed to protest me giving up my pants. When she saw the large gashes and massive bruises on my legs, from the pounding they'd taken in the surf, her face drew into a pained expression.

"Oh, Daddy, those are awful!"

"I didn't want you to see them," I said. The sores oozed red in their centers but had turned purple around the edges. The worst was a wound on my right knee that had cut deep enough to expose the kneecap. The floatcoat had protected my upper body when the surge had thrown me against the rocks, but my legs had had little protection. Cindy turned away, and I removed my undershorts before putting on my pants and boots again.

"Here, put these on over the sweater," I told Jena, handing her the underwear. The outfit would have been comical under any other circumstances, but Jena gave no thought to her appearance, and it proved functional. I could see a smile playing around the corners of Randy's mouth and knew that he was getting ready to tease his younger sister. I caught his eye and shot him a glance cold enough to chill any such idea.

Cindy discovered that one of the gloves she had hung to dry had fallen into the coals and melted. The other was damaged but still usable. I started to reprimand her; it seemed criminal to have so little, and then to destroy part of it when everything was vitally needed. But how could you speak harshly to a person who was so unselfish and compassionate and who tried as hard as Cindy?

That day I told them, "If I die, don't just leave my clothes lying here; take them—boots, everything. Somebody else can use them. They won't be any good to me." Randy could wear my boots, Jena needed my pants and Cindy was to take whatever she might need.

Earlier that winter, when the family had been sitting around the woodstove one evening, I had lightly told the children that there would not be much of value for them when I died. After Randy quickly claimed the sailboat and Jena the floathouse, Cindy said she would be content with the large Japanese fishing float. But now I was serious. No one spoke for a long time afterward.

Next to the fire we had gathered a large pile of tangled fishnet, scraps of rope, pieces of plastic debris from the drift piles and anything else that might burn strongly and make a dark smoke. At the first sound of a plane, we intended to throw everything on the fire as a signal. Throughout the day, whenever anyone heard or imagined hearing a new sound, he or she would yell, "Listen!" The others would stop, frozen in place, to strain their hearing toward the sound. There was never anything more than the rising wind tearing at the weather-worn trees.

As it grew darker, we moved closer to the fire. The tide had risen to full again, and the water lapped against the shore just below our camp. With the moon on the wane, the tidal flow also lessened each day. The lower high tides left a band of open gravel with little or no snow next to the snowbank. Our zone of habitation increased as the tide fell but disappeared completely beyond the short stretch of beach we occupied.

As he sat by the fire, Randy tugged and pulled at his little green boots, trying to remove them, but the swelling made it impossible. His toes continued to ache, and he said they felt as though they were on fire. He had allowed them to thaw. Cindy tried helping him, to no avail. Finally he asked her to cut them off to relieve the pain. Using one of the broken fragments of the Cheez Whiz jar, Cindy sawed a ragged line down the front of each boot until they slipped off easily. He could still wear them, but they no longer closed. In the process she cut her finger. It seemed to be only a minor cut at the time.

"Your feet smell like they're rotting," Cindy told him. He removed his socks, and they could see dead flesh on his big toes, already beginning to slough away. His smaller toes ached too, but they didn't appear to have been damaged.

As darkness wrapped around our little camp, Randy, as usual, was up latest by the fire. We had difficulty getting comfortable. The shelter was cold, there wasn't enough room and we had no covers. We moved continuously in an effort to gain some small comfort, to get just a little sleep.

Once, when Cindy was sure that I was awake, she again brought up the plan she and Randy had discussed earlier in the day.

"No, we're going to stick together," I said. "As long as we're together, we're okay; we can help each other. If somebody gets separated, they don't stand a chance. I think the four of us will get there just as fast anyhow."

Cindy said no more about it. Later I spoke again. "Cindy, would you mind turning the other direction? Your clam breath is more than I can stand."

The situation was similar to complaints that the children had made about my oyster breath five years earlier. When doctors had diagnosed my arthritis as incurable, I had sought hopefully after cures not recognized by the medical profession. One such treatment was to rub the afflicted area with a substance called DMSO that passes readily through the skin and into the joints. It was approved for use on animals only, but I had managed to obtain some for myself. Each night Cindy would put on protective gloves to apply the substance to my back and shoulders. The relief was only temporary, and the one noticeable side effect was a strong breath resembling the smell of oysters.

The wind and snow began again in the night. The accumulation on the sail melted and dripped on us. Our constant moving dislodged the tent pole, collapsing the top onto us. My first thought was to rebuild the shelter, but the closeness of the sail against my body felt much more protective. I decided the tent idea had been wrong from the beginning. The fabric was more valuable lying directly on us, where it had some chance of retaining our body heat. Randy had found the same thing to be true the night before but, characteristically, had not wished to argue the issue, so he had not mentioned it when I told him to prop the sail up. We did not try again to build a shelter. It only created uncomfortable space that we could not heat.

FEBRUARY 18

When I awoke, the sky had cleared, lowering the temperature even further. I could see the north wind was still blowing strongly down the strait, but my mind was on another subject. I felt I had solved the problem of the raft. The idea had come to me sometime in the night, and I eagerly shared it with the others.

"Even if we could move those big logs, we don't want that kind of raft anyhow. We want one we can paddle, not a bunch of logs in the water. Let's just use those two long logs and put the Sport-Yak between them. All we need are some short crosspieces to hold the thing together."

As the tide receded that morning we roamed up and down the sunny beach, poking into the exposed edges of drift piles, picking out what we needed and talking casually to one another, feeling neither anxiety nor fear at our predicament. When we had assembled the rest of the materials, we rolled the two long logs into position on the tide flat in front of our camp. It would be almost five hours before the tide rose enough to float our creation.

The logs were rough spruce about ten inches in diameter at the thicker end and nearly twenty-four feet long. We laid them side by side, four feet apart, and put four crosspieces atop them. Randy worked at the stiff rope ladder to undo the splices he had so painstakingly made years earlier. He freed the rope rungs from one side only, leaving the short splices still hanging from the other side. The scraps of rope we found on the beach were tied together for lashing material. Near the narrow ends of the logs we fastened a weathered four-by-four post crosswise with rubber tubing. At midship a two-by-ten-inch plank was fastened with scraps of rope and left to extend a foot on each side. Behind the plank we lashed the Sport-Yak between the logs, using the grommet holes along the sides of the boat. Placing the plywood from the pilothouse atop two driftwood poles at the rear, we created a platform raised slightly above the Sport-Yak. We straightened the nails in the plywood and hammered them with rocks to hold the platform solidly to the poles. I called it "the poop deck," not just for nautical reasons but also because of the square hole in the center of the plywood.

We used every piece of rope we had found for lashing and saved the electrical wire for a painter, to tie the raft to shore when we stopped.

With our departure imminent, we threw the remaining wood, debris, tangles of net and rope scraps onto the fire in the hope that someone might see our signal. But as we watched the dark smoke rise, the wind came up and pulled it back into the trees, dissipating it through the dense forest.

As the tide began to pour onto the gravel flat through the narrow channels between the small islands, we loaded everything aboard. I would have liked to have had time to test the raft's buoyancy and strength before we got on, but I was not overly concerned. It appeared seaworthy, and we really had little choice. We laid the sail across the floor of the Sport-Yak and the poop deck, with extra fabric at both ends brought back over for protection. The foam pads we would use as cushions, mattresses or for cover, depending on the circumstances. Small items were stored under the piece of plywood in the bottom of the punt.

Cindy and Jena left camp reluctantly. Even though the temperature had stayed below freezing, the bright sun and our windless location on the gentle gravel beach offered more comfort than the frigid water. The prospect of setting out on that sea in a raft made being stranded on the barren beach seem only an inconvenience that would surely be overcome.

# 5

# THE RAFT

As the tide rose around the raft, we smiled nervously, watching the water line rise on the logs. The thing was bound to float eventually, but we were concerned that the logs would be too far under water, leaving not enough freeboard.

When the water neared the tops of the logs, we felt the scrape of gravel and then movement.

"It floats!" Cindy yelled.

Quickly we took our positions. I was at the front of the Sport-Yak, with Cindy and Randy side by side behind me, each holding an oar for paddling. Jena was lying under the sail atop the raised platform at the rear. Cindy and Randy pushed off against the gravel bottom and began paddling toward the six-foot gap between the two closest islands. With the tide still flowing into the cove, they had to struggle against it through the channel. We turned north and followed the shoreline. The tide would soon turn, and we would be less affected by its adverse current close to shore; we would also keep out of the cold wind that funneled down the center of the channel.

The long sleek raft moved surprisingly well and was easy to maneuver, gliding smoothly through the water with only normal paddling effort.

"We're going faster than we could walk," Jena observed.

Randy and Cindy switched round the three remaining gloves to save their hands from blistering. Randy tried to adjust his paddling to match Cindy's and to keep the raft traveling in a straight path, but he was impatient and occasionally blurted out, "Can't you paddle any harder than that?" Jena and I relieved Cindy occasionally so she could rest, but even the three of us, taking turns, were hard pressed to match Randy's strong effort.

As we saw how well the raft moved, our spirits lifted considerably. One of the last items I had asked Randy to find before leaving camp was a long pole suitable to use as a mast. Once the weather changed it would be a simple matter to raise a corner of the sail and catch the south wind up Kaigani Strait. The problem of reaching Rose Inlet began to seem less imposing.

North and west of us the twin peaks of a distant mountain on Dall Island glowed a rosy white in the fading sun.

"Do you remember that peak, Randy?" I asked.

Randy stared at it awhile before he answered. "That's the one at the end of Waterfall Bay, isn't it?"

"What's on the east side of the island, across from Waterfall Bay? Remember when we were anchored in the bay that time, and you said you could walk across the island in a few hours?"

Randy nodded his head in recognition and smiled, still keeping his rhythm on the oar. "Rose Inlet," he said.

To Jena, the white of the mountain was just a blur on the horizon. "How far is it?" she asked.

"What would you guess, Randy?" My eyes were not much better than Cindy's, without glasses, and I had to rely on my son's judgment.

"Twenty miles. I don't know, maybe a little more."

We had made our first visit to Rose Inlet in the summer of 1977. The chart said only ABANDONED CANNERY SITE, leaving so much unsaid that we could not resist the temptation to go the extra six miles out of our way and investigate.

The day was bright and sunny, the breeze was light and only a gentle swell crossed the surface of Tlevak Strait. The children had a large buoy tied on a line hanging from the highest point of the rigging. One of them would sit astraddle the buoy, and the others would start it swinging. As the buoy swung from side to side, the boat would roll with its rhythm and increase the arc.

Randy was on the swing, Cindy and Jena were on the deck nearby, Margery was at the tiller and I was in the pilothouse with her. Absentminded Cindy had her attention distracted. As Randy crossed the deck at the bottom of his gigantic uncontrolled sweep, she stepped in the path of the buoy and was bowled over the rail of the boat into space.

Margery screamed, and I looked forward to see Cindy sitting at the top of her trajectory with knees bent, legs spread and eyes of unbelievable size. She immediately dropped from view past the side of the boat.

The keel of the *Home* was long and heavily ballasted, to keep wind pressure in the sails from turning it over, and also to aid in steering a true course. Though it was necessary for sailing, this feature precluded quick turns and easy maneuvering.

I grabbed the tiller from Margery and swung it to start

a turn. Though we were traveling on engine power, the heavy boat moved on through the water for some distance before responding. I brought the boat around, returned and stopped it with the bobstay from the bowsprit close enough for Cindy to grab and climb aboard.

"You just kept going and going," Cindy said. "That water's awful cold. It was hard not to panic."

After this incident, we devised a life ring with an attached line for use should we ever have anything similar happen. Our visits to Rose Inlet seemed destined to be eventful.

We had been traveling for several hours. The current flowing up the strait weakened as the tide peaked and would soon be flowing against us. Ahead, a hooklike point jutted out, and beyond it I could see small waves blowing down the channel from the north. I felt we should find a stopping place and directed Randy closer to shore so we could begin searching for a night camp. For ourselves, we would need a supply of wood and protection from the wind. For the raft, a steeply sloping beach would help keep it from going aground as the tide fell.

The deepest recess of the cove behind the rocky hook met all these requirements. The southern exposure that provided the driftwood could also mean misery should the weather shift in the night, but to face the chill north wind was a greater evil. We put ashore at the edge of a steep-faced rock shelf one hundred feet from the beach. It looked like the bare shelf flooded at higher tides but it was now exposed. We carried our sail and pads over the slick dark rocks to a band of gravel bordering the snow. In a futile gesture of shelter, the bare gnarled limbs of a dormant alder hung over our campsite.

Large logs were plentiful, but smaller firewood was very difficult to find under the snow. We built our fire between two huge parallel logs that reached above our heads when we were sitting down. The space was not large enough for all of us to sleep side by side, so we arranged the sail for two sets of sleepers lying head to head. The warmth of the fire reflected back and forth between the logs, giving us the most comfort we had yet had. We lay back against the logs to soak in the heat and get some much-needed rest.

"What are you thinking about, Randy?" Cindy asked.

Randy smiled broadly. "Well, you know those cinnamon rolls we had on the boat? I sure wish I'd eaten them before the boat went down."

"You know what I was thinking about?" she countered. "Remember the blueberry pie that I forgot to put on the boat when we left the floathouse? I wonder if it'll still be okay when we get home."

"It's been cold the whole time. It should keep," he assured her.

"I don't think you guys should be talking about food," I broke in. "It doesn't do you any good—just makes you hungrier."

"Oh, Daddy," Cindy said, "It won't hurt us. It's something to talk about."

No one spoke for several minutes. Finally I broke the silence. "You know, we were close enough to shore, at times before the boat sank, that we could have thrown those cans of beans up onto the beach."

"Daddy, you said . . ."

"I know. I won't any more. I was just thinking."

"Do you suppose there will be anyone at Rose Inlet, Daddy?" Jena asked.

"It really won't make much difference," I replied. "The CB is there, and Jim and Sondra said that Pat Tolson would be back in a few days, so he'll probably be there."

Randy got up several times to push the raft away from the rocks and to check the wire line to be certain it was tied securely. As it grew colder, we huddled between the logs and covered ourselves with the foam pads and several layers of sail. Either our bodies were adjusting or the shelter was much more efficient; we were able to get some true sleep for what seemed to be the first time since the wreck, four nights before.

## FEBRUARY 19

I roused the children early in the morning, before daylight, and after only a short warm-up next to the fire, we were back on the raft. As Randy and Cindy half carried, half dragged the heavy sail to the raft, they argued over which one it was. Cindy thought it was one of our big genoas because of its bulk. Randy believed it to be the storm jib because of the heavy cloth. (Although Cindy conceded, she was later proved to be correct.)

After the ease with which we had traveled the previous evening, I was anxious to be under way once more. I guessed that those few hours of travel the day before had taken us perhaps two miles up the beach. But we would eventually need to cross Kaigani Strait to the Dall Island side. I wanted to have that behind us as soon as possible. Once the south wind started, the crossing would be more dangerous.

The stars faded and the horizon lightened as we pushed away from shore. As we moved farther from camp, the north wind grew stronger. By the time we reached the rocky point, the wind and waves caught us full force. Stinging cold brought tears to our eyes. The waves washed easily over the logs and against the Sport-Yak wetting our clothes through the sail, making the cold bitter. Spray froze and cracked in the folds of the sail covering our bodies. Even with the tide still favoring us as we came abreast of the jutting point, we could not move against the freezing wind.

The point was still abreast of us, yet we had paddled hard for almost an hour. Cindy and Randy kept pulling at the oars, but soon Cindy's stroke slowed and Randy laid down his oar and shoved his hands into his armpits, doubling over from the pain in his freezing fingers. His face was blotched red from exertion; his eyes ran freely.

I gave the only order I could. "Let's go back. There's no sense in this. We can't fight against it; we have to go with it."

As we paddled back to our camp, we could see the smoke still rising from the fire. We crawled into the shelter of the logs and lay back. By the time we woke, the sun was already high in the southern sky.

It was the fifth day since the shipwreck, the sixth since we had really had a meal. My Pepto-Bismol bottle had long ago lost all flavor, but I continued to fill it with snow, and after leaving it beside the fire to warm, I drank small amounts. My stomach had calmed considerably although the contractions still occurred at irregular intervals.

I stood next to the fire in the sunlight, coughing, and then breathed in hard through my nostrils to clear a congestion deep in my sinuses. Suddenly, as the cold air met the burning nasal passages, my suffering made sense to me. I blurted out to the children, "My God, I've had the flu. That's what's been wrong with me. The upset stomach, weakness, burning sinuses—that's what it's been—the damn flu!" I had made a trip to Craig the day before we left for Prince Rupert, to take care of the mail, buy a few groceries and visit Margery. Many children were absent from school because of an epidemic of intestinal flu. The timing was right. I had caught it then.

Cindy smiled. "We all knew you were sick."

"Yes, I've had the flu the whole time, but it should have about run its course by now. I'll be getting better soon." The revelation was astounding to me.

My hopes for reaching Rose Inlet within a day or two had been dashed, but I was not yet worried. I told the children we would have to move with the tides until the north wind had stopped. If the wind blew too strongly, we would wait. There would be no sense in fighting the cold when a weather change was long overdue and we could expect warmer temperatures and southerly winds at any time.

Toward midday, the tide reached low water. Soon the current would start running north through the strait. If we were to make another attempt at going on today, now was the time to begin. The sheltered location of our camp made it difficult to judge the wind except to watch the rollers far out in the center of the channel. Randy could see whitecaps offshore, but partly out of something to do, he said he was going to walk to the point to check the wind. Low tide would make the several hundred yards of beach easier, and Cindy volunteered to go with him.

When they reached a level beach connected to the rock of the point itself, the warmth of the sun was so pleasant, and their feet were hurting so, they sat down on the gravel and wriggled into its surface to make hip holes. Except for the north wind in the trees far above them, and the occasional metallic chinking of gravel, the beach was totally silent. Lying back with his eyes closed to the bright sun, Randy finally spoke. "If I took the Sport-Yak by myself, I could be there tomorrow."

"Daddy said he thought we should stick together."

"I know, but it's going to take us a week at this rate."

"This weather's going to turn southeast pretty soon. It won't blow from the north much longer."

Again Randy let it go.

The snow had been blown or washed away from most of the point, and when Cindy and Randy reached the end they saw an iron post cemented into a hole in the rock. An iron loop had been welded at its top.

"Look at this, Randy."

"It's a bollard," he said. "The seiners use them to tie off the other end of their nets. I don't think they're legal anymore. It must be an old one."

Still, this sign of civilization excited them and lessened the strangeness of the beach. Before returning to camp, they picked several handfuls of large mussels from the rocks around the point.

Later in the afternoon, they started back again to check the wind once more and to find more mussels, but this time Cindy's weakness overcame her and she stopped short of the point. Her feet were hurting more each day, and her saltwater-soaked corduroy jeans had rubbed the skin from both knees. While Randy continued on, Cindy lay in a large crevice among the rocks, out of the wind, and rested. It was the first time she had felt too tired to move. She picked a small piece of green seaweed from the rocks and chewed on it tentatively. The longer she chewed the stronger it tasted, and eventually she spat it out.

When they got back, Randy reported to me that the winds beyond the point were even stronger than before. I was not surprised and had already decided to spend the night, rather than try to fight our way north any more that day. Everyone accepted my decision. The bitter cold of our early morning effort made the fire and our sheltered camp a most welcome alternative.

As the sun set behind Dall Island and the temperature fell, we built up the fire and settled into the space between the logs. Cindy was obviously deep in thought. I could tell that something was troubling her, so I asked her what it was, and once again she asked if it wouldn't be better to send someone ahead. My answer was the same: We would stick together. I didn't think Randy could paddle the punt into that cold north wind. And as soon as it died down, we could all move with the raft.

Randy laid out the mussel shells next to the fire and gathered together what cooking equipment we had. There was the metal lid to the breakfast drink jar, a small alligator clip from the mast wire to use as a potholder and the yellow plastic kitchen container. He experimented with the roasted mussels by frying small pieces in corn oil and adding a pinch of spaghetti seasoning. The metal lid upset too often because of its small size, so he began to fry the mussels in the larger shells. The alligator clip became a tong to remove the sizzling meat. After he had prepared several mussels this way, each of his sisters took a turn at cooking. None of them balked any more at eating the entire mussel, even the bright orange parts, but with only a teaspoon of meat per sitting, there wasn't enough to even begin to satisfy their hunger and their talk soon turned to other foods.

"Every time I lick my fingers," Cindy said, "I think of that sticky apple fritter I ate in Prince Rupert."

"Why couldn't that container with the cinnamon rolls have made it ashore?" Jena moaned.

"I dreamed last night that I went to the floathouse," Randy said thoughtfully, "and I walked in and there was the blueberry pie still sitting there. There was no mold or anything."

"Didn't you eat any?" Jena asked.

"No, I just checked on it."

"All right, that's enough," I said firmly. "It's no help. I don't want you talking any more about food."

"Oh, Daddy . . ." Cindy started.

"No more," I said.

now he is just thinking
back in time till
Top of P.105

The reason for taking the children out of school that year and placing them on correspondence study was the uncertainty of their arrival and departure dates as well as the unpredictable time required for the trips to the orthodontist. But the same uncertainty and vagueness of our schedule would prevent anyone from reporting us missing. The implication of this did not seem troublesome to me at first. If we managed to rescue ourselves within a short time, it was of little importance. But now, after six days, I began to work at the problem in my mind. My older daughter Margery would expect me to visit her on the first Friday after we reached the floathouse, if the weather permitted.

"What day is it?" I said. "I mean, day of the week?"

"It's Monday," Cindy answered quickly. "We wrecked on the night of the fourteenth, on a Wednesday."

"Margery won't start worrying until next weekend. We've got four days to get to the cabin before she sounds the alarm."

"I'd like to think so," Cindy said, "but I don't think she will, not Margery. Daddy, we didn't even check out with customs. This time of all times!"

"I know, Cindy. We've been overdue before, but never this long."

In April, on the first trip to the orthodontist the previous year, Margery had taken our Volkswagen by ferry to Prince Rupert at the same time the other children and I had left by sailboat. We could not plan to use the ferry because it would be so complex, expensive and time consuming. Ketchikan is a stop on the main ferry line, but Prince of Wales Island is a branch line to one side and Prince Rupert to the other. The schedules don't coordinate and the ferries don't run daily. Then, to go as a "foot passenger" would require that we have a car at Craig, because the ferry terminal is thirty miles away on a gravel road. We would need another car at Prince Rupert because Terrace, where the doctor's office is, is ninety-six miles from the terminal there. Then we'd have to pay for food and lodging for the four of us for ten days to two weeks on every round trip. The children would not be able to do their schoolwork and the whole thing would be impossible. Instead, we stored our car in Prince Rupert at $15 a month and, using the sailboat to live in, we could make the round trip in five to eight days —usually. It was cost-effective and schoolwork could go on.

The first time we made the trip, because the weather seemed fair, I decided to head directly out to sea from Craig rather than to thread our way through the narrow rocky passage of the inside route. We would pass to the outside of Dall Island and enter Dixon Entrance from the ocean. The winds would be steadier for sailing, and we could also travel at night. According to my estimate, we should reach Prince Rupert in twenty-four hours, about the same time as Margery. We planned to leave the car in Prince Rupert for subsequent trips to Terrace, and Margery would return with us on the sailboat.

The weather did not cooperate. Halfway down the outside of Dall Island, several miles offshore, we encountered fog. At first we trusted to the compass heading and continued, but as the fog thickened I became worried and turned toward the island. With two children on the bow as lookouts, we approached the storm-ravaged cliffs of

Dall Island at a slow crawl. As we encountered the first reefs offshore we slowed even further, trying to peer through the dense fog, hoping to find the mouth of one of the several bays indenting the island's coastline. Luckily, we had met the island almost directly in front of a large cove, and after entering we identified it by its islands as Waterfall Bay, due west of Rose Inlet.

The fog held until the following morning, when a strong southeast wind arose. We were able to follow the coastline out of the wind to Cape Muzon, on the southern tip of the island. Beyond the cape, Dixon Entrance was in full gale, and we retreated to Wolk Harbor, just north of the cape, to wait out the storm. The cove offered perfect protection from the southeast winds, but as the storm moved inland the winds shifted, coming directly into the harbor just after midnight. The boat began pitching violently, and I could feel the anchor dragging in the soft bottom. There was only one hope—to pull anchor and run north.

Outside the harbor, the seas were higher than anything we had ever seen. The waves crashed brutally against the upper structure of the cabin as we motored at top speed toward Security Cove, six miles away. A lone light flashed at Point Cornwallis; otherwise we were surrounded by darkness and storm. When I saw that the Sport-Yak was being torn loose from its lashings, I fought my way on deck to save it. Randy stayed at the tiller, trying desperately to steady the boat while I was out on deck. As I returned, he said angrily, "I wouldn't have done that. I would have let it go. It wasn't worth the risk."

I shook off my fear and said, "We might need it someday."

We waited out the storm in Security Cove and arrived in Prince Rupert nearly three days late. Margery had been very worried, but she had not contacted anyone. She would no doubt remember that trip and hold out even longer this time.

The hours of lounging close to the flames lulled us into a strange sense of security. Jena said she wished she would never have to leave the fire. Besides her fear of water since the shipwreck, the feeling of comfort and warmth pulled her thoughts inward. She talked very little. I also felt the laziness and wasn't aroused until I felt stabbing pain in my feet; I had kept them by the fire for too long. I arose from the reflecting oven of the logs and shoved my boots deep into the cold dry snowbank behind the camp until the pain subsided. The damage had already been done. I knew I could not let the flesh thaw, not yet.

FEBRUARY 20

The north wind increased in the night and began reaching over the sheltering point to beat directly onto our camp from above. By morning the wind had dropped, but it still continued to fill the channel with row after row of whitecaps from the north. We could only wait. The clear, cold sky continued, and Cindy and Jena's lassitude became stronger, keeping them close to the fire, lying back in the bright sun. Only Randy roamed the beach, collecting more mussels and wood for the fire. Once, during the day, we were sure we heard the deep throb of a large diesel motor coming closer. Cindy took off her bright blue floatcoat and turned it inside out to expose the red lining, but the sound came no closer and eventually faded.

Toward midday, the channel calmed and Randy made several trips to the raft, pushing it off the rocky shelf into deeper water as the tide fell; it had to be ready when we were. His feet were swollen and painful in his tight boots —even with their slit fronts. But he was stronger than the rest of us and tended both fire and raft without complaint. He spoke of how easy it would be to catch all we wanted to eat—if we just had a single hook and a length of line. We knew that, all along the shoreline, bottom fish of every description were feeding greedily on anything that came within their reach. It would be so good to pick the white flesh from a whole rockfish after it had cooked in the coals. Unlike the girls and me, the wait on the beach, knowing that the cabin was perhaps only fifteen miles away, tortured Randy. He mentioned the dish of almonds and raisins our hosts had placed on the table the night we had stopped in Rose Inlet. That was the first thing he would eat.

Near sundown the wind decreased and the channel smoothed. The tide was rising. We could wait no longer. We would travel at night. We loaded the raft, got aboard and shoved off. The sun dipped below the mountains that rose steeply on the opposite side of the channel. Caught in the incoming current with only a light breeze opposing us, we quickly left the camp and the bollard point behind.

After seeing the strength of the north wind in the channel, I thought it best to cross while the wind allowed and directed Randy to begin angling for the opposite shore. Perhaps we could work our way slowly up the shore of Dall Island even if the north wind continued. To be on the same island as our objective would be some progress. Kaigani Strait narrowed perceptibly ahead of us, from approximately two miles wide at our present location to less than half that distance farther up the channel. We kept the snowy brilliance of the double-pronged peak behind Rose Inlet in sight, using it not only as a directional marker but as a goal to urge us on. Randy had chosen the downwind side of the raft for paddling. His extra strength was needed to hold the raft in position as it moved slowly across the strait to the dark forests of Dall Island. A lone wolf gave a long clear call from Long Island as if mourning the loss of companions.

Cindy and Randy rotated their three good gloves at regular intervals. They also changed oars from time to time. The hand grip had been snapped from one oar in the surf when the *Home* went down, making it hard to hold firmly. Their hands were puffy and whitish from the constant contact with water, icy wood and wet clothing. Small sores from their first night on the beach refused to heal and burned continually from the saltwater. Blisters formed and broke only to form again in deeper layers of skin. The cut on Cindy's hand, from slitting her brother's boots, had not healed and was very painful. As Cindy grew weaker in the endless sweep and pull of the oar, I tried to relieve her. I could not paddle in the normal manner by strongly flexing my arms and shoulders, so I would lean forward, bending at the waist, then lean back with my body weight against the oar. It was not nearly as effective, and I soon grew tired.

Cindy's stomach muscles grew tighter and seized her body with cramps as she struggled to keep pace with her brother. She mentioned it not in complaint but only as the reason she did not keep up. Randy was able to kneel hour after hour without shifting position. Cindy's knees were rubbed raw by the salt in her jeans. She tried to sit to paddle, but the downward slant of the plywood in the Sport-Yak made it impossible to reach forward in her strokes. Eventually she settled on a cross-legged squat that lifted her high enough and also kept her knees from touching. Randy glowered at her constant shifting and paddled in spite of her pauses, which forced Cindy to resume more strongly in order to bring the raft into line.

There was no exchange of talk, only an occasional sentence spoken to no one in particular, followed by long periods of silence. It was always Cindy who broke the silence, trying to make conversation, though the rest of us seldom responded. In spite of her weakness and our difficult situation, she continually found reason for optimism. It was only when she mentioned food that the other two children would join in.

"Just think," she said, "when we get back we can buy all new things for the kitchen, new pots and pans, and plates, and silverware. We'll have everything new. We can buy all new clothes, too."

Jena's disembodied voice came from under the sail at the rear of the raft. "I don't have anything to wear. It was all on the boat."

Hours later, as we approached the dark shores of Dall Island, their thirst became as strong as their hunger. Cindy spoke again. "You know what I'd like, Daddy,"

"No, what?" I responded, expecting it to be some kind of food.

"A Miller."

"You mean one of those moths?" I asked incredulously, looking toward her.

"No, a Miller High Life, the Champagne of Bottled Beer!"

We all laughed, and then the raft became silent again.

In the night, ahead of us, the shoreline retreated into a large bay with a small island stretching lengthwise across its mouth. We gained on its dark presence slowly. As well as weakness, we were also fighting the current as it swept southward down the channel with the changing tide. That meant we had paddled six hours. Even though we had been traveling diagonally to the west as well as to the north, I guessed that we had gained at least five miles. Together with our gain on Saturday afternoon, we should be almost halfway there. If the wind cooperated, we should reach Rose Inlet by the following evening.

"Pull in behind the island," I said. "Start looking for a camp."

The bay side of the long narrow island would give us protection from either a north or south wind, but as we paddled its snowy shore we found only steep rock and dense forest. There was no possible camp or accessible wood supply in its entire length. Another half mile to the north, the dark point at the entrance to the bay began again, but there was no guarantee that we would find a more hospitable site. Though neither Cindy nor Randy had complained, I had no heart to push them any further. We decided to spend the rest of the night aboard the raft. In another six hours it would be daylight, the tide would be in our favor again for a few hours and the raft would be loaded and ready to go.

Randy went ashore on the island and picked through icy rocks in the dark to find one to bring back for a suitable anchor. We paddled a short distance from shore and Randy dropped his rock anchor over the side, but the thirty feet of electrical cord to which he had tied it went slack as the rock reached its end and slipped free without finding bottom. Randy said nothing but paddled the raft to the island again. He had soaked his feet trying to jump to shore the first time, so this time he saved his energy and waded ashore in the icy water. He groped among the rocks for several minutes until he found one with a narrow waist to prevent the wire from slipping loose again.

Staying closer to shore than before, Randy dropped the

rock and the anchor held. Jena stayed by herself on the four foot square of plywood, keeping her body curled around the foot-square hole in its center. Her fear of sliding off the edge into the dark water was stronger than her need for sleep. Cindy and Randy lay along the outside of the Sport-Yak, with me in the middle facing in the opposite direction. We shared less than three feet of space between us. Our backs sagged to the wet floor of the punt, our heads and feet were raised awkwardly by the bow and stern. We had some of the sail under us and some folded back over the top. The foam pads were soaked and ineffective. We were all cold. After six hours of constant paddling, and being in cramped positions, we were seized by muscle cramps as we tried to sleep. In such tight quarters, every movement brought a protest from someone. We suffered each cramp as long as we could before stretching to relieve it, and we slept miserably—if at all.

## FEBRUARY 21

At first light, Randy pulled up the anchor rock and untied it, dropping it back into the water, and he and Cindy paddled away from the nameless island in the unknown cove. The wrenching pain of reaching forward and pulling back with the oars was almost a relief to them. The returning current of high water pulled against us, and as we emerged from behind the mouth of the bay, we were met once again by a stiff north wind rolling a heavy chop down the strait. The sun came up bright at our backs but was powerless against the freezing wind stinging our hands and faces.

One mile distant a small bight recessed behind a short rocky point, and we hugged the shoreline, striving to reach its shelter. Our progress was painfully slow. Rocks and logs on the beach beside us mocked our slow pace. Waves threw an almost continual sheet of spray over the front of the raft into the Sport-Yak. The square hole in the afterdeck funneled the heavy water into a small geyser, gusting and collapsing beside Jena at the back. I leaned hard to the side, trying to lift the outside log of the raft enough to break the waves before they struck the captive punt. No raft logs showed above the choppy water. We were only a strange canvas wrapping, with arms and faces emerging from its sides, moving against tide and wind.

As we closed on the rocky point, its shelter mercifully broke the wind and stirred the current into a back eddy, pulling the raft closer. There was no question about continuing; it wasn't possible. The raft bumped against a rock wall, and slowly each of us climbed from our canvas shroud and lay down against the sun-warmed rocks. We tied down the raft and pushed it away from shore, ready to leave when conditions changed. The rush of wind in the heaving growth of evergreens overhead told us all we needed to know, and we slept.

When she woke, Cindy could feel only pain and weakness in her body. It was more than stiff joints and muscles, more than sores that didn't heal. She explained it to us later as a web or net that confined her physical presence, consuming her strength and sapping her will. She said she felt as if she could lie on the warm rocks in the sun forever. The snow above our heads dripped slowly from an icy line where it met the warm rock. The wind was a hushed roar, like the sound of a seashell placed against the ear. The scraping of our jackets against the rock reminded us that we were there also.

The tide receded, and soon Randy became restless. I

joined him at the point, and together we looked out at the
strait. "It's hard to believe that the wind can stay so cold
and always from the north. We would expend all of our
energy and freeze to death trying to buck it. Let's move a
little bit farther back in the cove and find a place for a
fire. Maybe it will quiet down again this evening."

I called to the girls to board the raft. They rose wearily.
Aboard the raft, Cindy paddled without interest in the
shoreline; she seemed almost irritated to have had to
leave the warm rocks. The point that formed the small
cove was low, with deep cracks that funneled the biting
wind into the bay. About two hundred yards into the bight,
a sloping beach of chunky dark rock offered the only sem-
blance of a camp. We beached the raft and climbed
ashore and Jena sat down right there. Wood was scarce,
but Randy picked through snowy drift piles and eventually built up a small supply.

I noticed a change in Cindy, a withdrawn moodiness.
"Cindy, why don't you go find a creek and fill my bottle
and the bowl for us?" (This place did not have a stream
nearby, as most of the other campsites had had.)

Cindy balked and then, on the verge of tears, shuffled
down the beach, trying to walk among the loose rocks on
the outside edges of her feet. The bottoms of her feet had
become increasingly sore, as if the flesh were raw under the cover of skin. The first trickle of water she found
was encased in ice, and she tried in vain to break
through to the underlying stream before giving up to
search for another.

The fire was sending a swirl of smoke downwind by the
time Cindy returned, and she lay down in the rocks beside it. Jena had not moved from where she had first settled down.

I knew that Randy would soon want to load the raft
and try to travel, so I pointed to the line across our little

bay where the white-crested chop merged with the calm water in front of our camp. "We know how rough it is out in the strait now," I said. "As long as this little cove looks as it does now, there's no need to go back to the point to check on conditions there." He never answered, but just walked off toward the lower beach. I joined the girls by the fire.

A short while later, Randy walked back to camp from the tidal area with cupped hands, dumped a small pile of steamer clams into the rocks beside the fire, turned and walked back to the beach. Without talking, he communicated his growing irritation that the rest of us seemed to be doing nothing to help ourselves. The clams were quite small, ranging from fingernail size to that of a half dollar. Though I had thought that nothing could move them from the fire, both Cindy and Jena got up to follow Randy. The rocks of the beach were large, but between them some muddy gravel held a few small clams. After using a stick to scratch the surface, Randy would sift through the watery depression with his fingers, searching the mud for the tiny mollusks. Cindy and Jena went to holes that Randy had started and stirred the icy water with their fingers, raking out clams that Randy had missed. Their fingers grew bitterly cold, and soon they could no longer feel whether they were touching clams, rocks or anything at all. They carried back their handful of clams while Randy continued the hunt until he was forced to the upper beach by rising water and darkness.

The small white butter clams more closely resembled those that we gathered regularly near the floathouse. They were far more appetizing than the dark, strong-tasting mussels the children had eaten at the last camp. They were no longer concerned with whether the clams were thoroughly cooked but ate them as soon as the heat of the fire steamed the shells open. They ate steadily until the entire supply was gone, and then they picked at the remaining shells for small morsels they had missed earlier. It's doubtful that any of them had more than one good mouthful.

My case of the flu must have about run its course. The aroma of steaming clams actually smelled good. I tried eating two of the smaller ones that Randy offered me, but my stomach was not ready to accept solid food. I chewed steadily until I had swallowed most of the juices and then spat out the stringy meat. I then suffered more frequent stomach contractions throughout the night.

With the water gone and no one willing to find more, the children began eating snow to quench the thirst brought on by the salty clams. I warned them all, "Don't eat too much of that. Your body has to work to melt it. It will just make you colder."

The wind grew stronger and, with our wood supply low, we retired to the sail early. The rocky cut behind our camp allowed the stronger gusts to blow directly on us during the night, scattering the coals and ashes of our fire.

## February 22

At daybreak, Randy and I rose first and verified that the wind blowing into our camp was indeed much stronger out in the strait.

I took the piece of quarter-inch plywood and stood it on its long edge in the snowbank above the fire. It served effectively as a windshield for a small area, diverting the steady wind but having little effect on the stronger gusts.

Randy spent the day gathering wood at high water and small clams at low water. He kept the raft pushed away from the shore, ready if we should need it. Increasingly,

Jena pulled deeper inside herself, and Cindy's sense of limbo made her as lethargic as her sister. Lying quietly by the fire seemed to take all the energy they had. Hunger was progressing into starvation. Damn the wind!

The afternoon low tides had been dropping lower each day and the high water of early morning moved farther toward the snowline. The greater fluctuation would increase the flow of the current in the channel. As the tide receded toward evening, Randy gathered clams and watched the rolling waves in the strait, looking for even a slight change in the wind. The peaks of the waves no longer showed white tops, but even if the current proved stronger than the opposing wind, the waves were still too high for travel.

Randy was able to find enough clams to fill the yellow container. The smell of the clams no longer revolted me, and I moved closer as the children began to eat. They ate more slowly and more methodically, stretching their supply into the night. Eight days after the wreck and nine days since my last meal, I was finally able to overcome the resistance in my throat and swallow the meat I chewed. I ate six one-inch clams, the meat from each the size of a small grape. This was less than half of what the children ate, but I could manage no more. Afterward, I drank warm water from my Pepto-Bismol bottle to calm the reaction in my stomach.

As if to raise the sagging spirits of his sisters, Randy talked more than usual while he ate. To him it seemed obvious that with the sailboat gone we would move the floathouse back to town and he could go to high school in Craig. He mentioned the spring prom and even told his sisters whom he would take. The idea of living in town once again aroused Cindy, and she too talked of how much fun it would be to see her friends and go back to school.

I had said nothing to them of the future after we reached safety, and when I heard their discussion I interrupted. "I wasn't planning on moving the floathouse. There's got to be a way to finish your dental work. You two younger kids are about through anyway—one more trip might do it—and Cindy should have her braces off before summer is over. Next fall is soon enough for town and school."

Cindy smiled cautiously and stared at me. "You're kidding, aren't you, Daddy?"

"No. We're not going to just forget the trips to Rupert."

"Well, I am," Randy blurted out, and rather than risk further confrontation he walked away from the fire.

When he returned to camp, we had crawled under the sail for the night. He lay down next to Jena on the outside and curled up tightly to warm himself. Jena moved closer to press against him, trying to absorb his heat. She said he must have a special mechanism of retaining his body heat that kept her from feeling any warmth, no matter how close she got. She turned in the other direction and moved close to her sister.

## FEBRUARY 23

Whipped by strong winds during the night, the fire had burned itself out by morning. I gathered fresh wood together and attempted to start it once more. I splashed it with some of the contents of the plastic jug, but as I lit a match, the wood sputtered and the flame died. I tilted the jug and stared into it. As I feared, most of the remaining liquid was rusty brown water, lying under a thin layer of diesel. I cursed myself for not siphoning off the top of the boat's metal fuel tank instead of letting the hose rest on the bottom, where water must have collected.

Our experiments with cooking had shown us that the corn oil itself was flammable, though not as effective as diesel. There was less than half a gallon of corn oil remaining, and I used it sparingly to get the fire going.

As I sat in front of the fire that afternoon, looking at the three gloves propped up to dry, I had an idea. I removed my floatcoat and the gray cotton sweatshirt that I wore under it. The sweatshirt had a thin foam innerlayer that let it retain some warmth, even when wet. Laying a sleeve over a rounded rock I picked up a smaller stone with a ragged edge and started pecking on the sleeve. Soon it was severed, and I handed it to Cindy, who had been staring in disbelief. "It's another glove, sweetheart. It looks like you'll be needing it."

The wind continued to gust throughout the day, but late in the afternoon, as we waited for the falling tide to expose the clam beds, the wind dropped suddenly. There was no rejoicing or excitement among us, only a numb release of tension. With the last rays of sun glowing golden on the snowy hillside of Long Island across the strait, we loaded the raft and pushed off.

My earlier optimism about reaching the cabin had been cruelly frustrated by the constant north wind. I had supposed that hunger would not be a factor in our ability to survive, but now, after nine days on the beach in below-freezing cold and ten days of very little food, I could see the effects on the children. Even Randy's activity had slowed to stumbling and plodding. Out of personal choice, I have fasted a few times, once for nine days, but I was in the warmth of the floathouse and could voluntarily reduce my physical activity during a fast. The children had never joined me in those purifying rituals.

From what I knew of fasting, I did not think it wise for children to even attempt to fast. A constant supply of nutrients was needed for growth and to fuel their higher metabolic rate. Without food, they would begin to suffer much sooner than adults. I needed no books to tell me what I could see at first hand. We had to reach Rose Inlet soon. The children would not have the strength to continue much longer.

In the slack water against the light breeze, Cindy and Randy struggled to keep a rhythm to their paddling, but as the tide began flooding and the raft gained speed, their muscles limbered. The nearby beach moved behind us much faster than we could have walked, even in the open stretches, when we were stronger. It was heartening, and the kids gladly gave what strength they had.

Dark fell as we moved out farther into the channel. We passed a large bay to the west and entered into the narrowest section yet. I tried desperately to picture the strait in my mind. I had studied the chart many times, but I had always looked on the Cordova Bay side of Long Island. From memory I knew Rose Inlet was west of the northern tip of Long Island, and also that one or more islands stood close to the end of Long Island on the west side. Rose Inlet itself was not entirely visible from the outside, and only by traveling past the small islands in its mouth, and around a sharp bend, could the two-mile fjord be seen. The mountains rose to over two thousand feet directly behind the inlet, so that passing boats had no indication of its presence without a map or chart.

"Start looking for some small islands on the other side, Randy. Mostly keep an eye on Long Island. I want to know when we reach its north end." I removed the sail to look out occasionally, but for the most part I stayed covered. Randy could see much better anyway and would describe it to me.

The current began increasing dramatically. The raft sped faster, as if we had entered a swift river.

"We're really moving," Cindy yelled. Jena rose up briefly from under the sail and was startled to see white clam shells under the water racing away behind us.

In spite of the easier paddling, Cindy could barely hold her oar. "Jena, couldn't you paddle for a while?" she asked.

Jena switched positions with Cindy and paddled weakly with the current.

"As soon as we get back," Randy announced hopefully, "I'm taking everyone to Ruth Ann's for dinner. You can order anything you want."

Soon afterward, Randy shook me to rouse me from under the sail. "The channel's getting wider and there are two islands on the other side."

I raised up briefly but could not see in the darkness as well as Randy could. "Watch for the end of Long Island," I said and covered up with the sail, again to escape the stiffening north breeze.

As the wind grew stronger, the tide began to slacken. The channel widened considerably until it no longer pinched the flowing current. Jena could not keep up with Randy's pace and began to complain about the cold and her discomfort. Cindy brusquely resumed her place in the Sport-Yak, sending Jena to the rear. "None of us has got it easy," Cindy lashed out at her.

I stayed quiet a while, and then I too admonished my younger daughter. "Jena, if all of us don't do our part, we're not going to make it. We can't spend all of our time taking care of you." But the words had little effect on her. She felt she had already been doing all she could.

The stars faded from the sky as thick clouds began to move in from the north. To escape the wind, we stuck close to the shore of Dall Island, but as we rounded a broad point, the north wind beat us toward the shore. Rather than turn back to find shelter, I told Randy to let the raft wash ashore. I suspected the tide had already turned, and to continue into the wind would be to risk losing everything.

The raft ground into the beach on a short stretch of moderately sloping rubble between two forested arms of dark rock that met the water. In the midst of the rubble, a single spire of rock rose sharply like a grim dark monument. Facing directly north, the broad front of the point had collected more than two feet of snow, which overhung the beach in a sharp-edged bank above the reach of the tide. A dead barkless tree with its limbs still intact stretched horizontally in the waves near the raft. We tried walking its slippery surface to shore but we slipped repeatedly into knee-deep water before reaching the higher rocks.

The children immediately went off in search of wood. The southern exposure of our other camps had always provided us with enough fuel for a fire, but this bleak northern beach had little. Returning to camp, Randy stared across the water to the other side of the strait. As the clouds rolled in thicker, he could see among them a long open stretch of water beyond Long Island. He had no way of knowing the angle at which he looked past the island, but the open water was definite.

He reported the view to me, and I looked up from my fire-building efforts to see nothing but clouds rolling through the darkness. Snow began blowing in on us as the fire repeatedly failed to catch. I used more and more of the corn oil, until very little remained. The fire was at last burning, but it would do us no good in our exposed location. We had no chance of drying any of our clothing, or even of feeling its warmth. Not having sufficient wood to keep it going, we left it, moving the pads and sail to a rocky section of beach above the tide line. It was hard work in the dark, over the slick uneven surface. We made our bed. We were all soaked from the waves washing against the Sport-Yak and lay tense and miserable as the cold wind howled across the sail over our heads.

"Today was Gran's birthday," Cindy said. "She would be expecting us to call. She'll be worried if she doesn't hear from us. Maybe she'll call somebody."

Cindy was talking about my mother in Oregon who would be seventy-seven years old that day. We were in touch by mail or telephone almost every week. By now, she had not heard from us for more than two weeks and perhaps would realize that it wasn't like us to miss her birthday.

"Who would she call?" I answered. "She'll wait to hear from us. But tomorrow's the weekend. If the weather's nice and we don't come into town, Margery's going to call the Coast Guard for sure."

"It won't do us any good, though; they'll only look on the Cordova Bay side of Long Island, where we usually travel."

"We made good time tonight. Rose Inlet can't be much farther."

Cindy shivered next to me and spoke distantly. "When we were building the raft and waiting in the sun, I wasn't afraid at all. I thought we could survive on the beach forever. But Daddy, this is bitter."

As usual, I couldn't sleep right away, so I used the time to mull over our situation and plan the next course of action. We had passed the narrows in Kaigani Strait, we had passed small islands, and Randy had seen open water beyond the north end of Long Island. We had put in six hours of travel between tide changes, and with the current we had sometimes gone as fast as two or three knots. We could be as far as twenty miles up the channel from Kaigani Point, or as little as fifteen. We had been too close to the island to be able to see the twin peaks any more, but we must be nearly abreast of them by now. Would the north wind continue? Or did the clouds mean a southeaster by morning? How much farther could it be? How much longer could the girls last? Since the *Home* entered the storm ten days before, the children had endured more hunger, cold, pain and fatigue than a person normally would in a lifetime, yet I had heard barely one word of complaint. They knew what had to be endured and what had to be done, and they did it. But Cindy's remark told what it was like. It was bitter.

I wrestled with my thoughts, and as I fell asleep, I thought, "Perhaps Randy and Cindy are right. Perhaps someone should go ahead."


FEBRUARY 24

In the gray morning light, I rose and looked into the spitting snow still borne by the north wind. The raft had become entangled in the branches of the tree where we had left it. It would be many hours before the tide rose high enough for us to free it. Across the strait toward Long Island clouds hung close to the dark rolling waves, blotting out everything. As I started walking toward the trees to the west, Randy joined me and stood beside me when I stopped at the small point of land to look farther up the beach. Hardly more than a mile away, a cluster of small islands sheltered an apparent indentation in the shoreline.

"Rose Inlet," I said softly.

"It sure looks like it," Randy added.

"Go untie the boat from the raft. We're going on ahead."

"What if they aren't there?"

"Jim and Sondra won't be there, and even if Tolson isn't either, we can call Hydaburg on the CB. Go on. I'll tell the girls."

Randy began freeing the six-foot punt from the raft as I walked back to Cindy and Jena. They were still partially asleep as I spoke to them. "Rose Inlet is right around the corner. Randy and I are going to take the Sport-Yak. We should be back with a skiff and outboard in three hours. If we aren't, you may have to move the sail up on the beach."

"Put some rice on to cook before you leave," Cindy said dreamily. "A big pot of rice."

I removed one of the thin foam pads from under the sail and left the other two for the girls. The plastic container of matches, the remaining corn oil, the diesel container and one onion I also left behind on a rock above the tideline where we had built the fire the night before. As we launched the skiff into the two-foot waves, I looked back briefly at the two forms lying motionless under the sail, and then began paddling toward the islands that had already disappeared in the low clouds. I had fought against splitting our group, but now it seemed merciful to spare the girls further misery. Randy and I envied them, under the sail, as we faced the icy wind and snow.

# 6

## THE CABIN

With the foam pad over our legs and lower bodies to fend off the constant wind-driven spray from the breaking waves, Randy and I paddled side by side. Within thirty minutes we had reached one of the small islands and pulled in to empty the water from the punt before going on. The shore behind the islands hooked inward, but I became less certain that the indentation hid the mouth of Rose Inlet. Then, as the clouds across the bay lifted momentarily, I saw for sure that we had been wrong. We could indeed see past the end of Long Island, but it was an oblique view to the northeast. We were still not abreast of the end. I recognized Aston and Grand islands off the north end of Long Island and estimated the distance at three miles.

"I still think we should go on," I told Randy, after we discussed our location.

"Shouldn't we tell them first?" Randy asked.

"It would make it that much longer before we got back here with the skiff. Let's keep going. It's got to be just around that point." I indicated the large peninsula jutting into the channel about two miles away. "Give me your oar. We can make better time if we shorten them, so we don't keep getting in each other's way."

I found a sharp rock and, placing each oar atop a large boulder, I pounded a ring around their circumference two feet below the ends. One oar broke in two easily as I bent it over the rock. The other took considerable pounding before giving way.

"These are different kinds of wood," I told Randy. "I think they pulled a fast one on you."

The care and thought Randy had put into the selection of the oars made no difference to him now. All that mattered were the oars themselves. The shorter oars were easier to use in the cramped boat, especially for my limited reach. We had reduced our options, however, since the oars would no longer be of much use on the raft. They were now just paddles.

The peninsula ahead of us blocked the worst of the north wind as long as we stayed close to the western shore. Farther out in the strait the waves broke heavily, pushing a surge of foam ahead of each crest. Even traveling with the current, we made slow progress bucking the stiff wind. The two miles took much longer than I had thought. Our arms hung heavily and our lungs burned with exhaustion as we touched shore just south of the point. The tide had risen almost to the snow line, but we found a small stream running from under the two-foot edge. Randy lay full length beside it, sucking at the icy water. I took some in my mouth and warmed it, then forced it into my stomach. We emptied the seawater from the Sport-Yak and began our assault on the exposed point ahead of us.

We planned to stay close enough to shore to swim to safety should the punt roll, but far enough out to avoid the steepening waves that broke against the beach. With our clothes streaming water, we no longer dodged the breaking waves but drove through them, letting the surge wash past us over the front of our tiny craft.

Our hopes had been dashed so often that the empty bay north of the point barely affected our morale.

"It's got to be the next one," I said, but the words no longer held conviction. We guided the boat in a wide arc into the bay, to gain protection from the wind as the next point loomed out of the snow ahead of us. The hours passed blindly; only the distance mattered. The tide zone along the beaches had disappeared and was now emerging again. The tide was going out. The three hours in the promise I had made to the girls had long since passed.

As we worked our way around the rocky point to the exposed north face, the wind became stronger, the waves larger. We were too weak to prevail against them. The beach we were now adjacent to was smooth and gently sloping for about half a mile.

"Relax, Randy. We can't make it this way anyhow. Let it wash us ashore and we can drag the Sport-Yak along the beach. We can't get any wetter than we are, and the sea isn't breaking big enough to hurt us."

A few minutes later our little punt was totally submerged as we were rolled roughly onto the gravel. The wind stung cruelly cold to our faces, lower bodies and legs. The floatcoats continued to do a good job of protecting our arms and upper bodies. We couldn't rest now. If we stopped for even a few minutes, we might not get started again.

We dragged the Sport-Yak clear of the surf and turned it up on edge to empty out the water, then wrung out the foam pad. I picked up the bow line and looped it over my shoulders, leaning forward to start the little boat sliding along the beach.

I was irritated that Randy was not beside me, pulling, and soon paused to speak to him about it. But when I turned, it was obvious that what I said would make little difference. He was a short distance behind, moving with difficulty and apparently near total exhaustion.

With the effects of the flu lessening, I had reached what I knew from fasting to be a plateau of energy, probably similar to a distance runner's second wind. Randy's young developing body had no such reserves to call on. We moved slowly up the beach, the plastic punt rattling over the rougher places and chattering on the smaller gravel.

To rest, and to allow Randy to catch up, I would lean a little less and let the Sport-Yak hold me up, then lean farther forward to start it moving again.

When we reached a section of beach too steep to traverse, we looked for the best place to float the punt again. We took some water aboard but managed to get beyond the steeper swells so we could again move parallel to the beach. After the walk it was a welcome change to kneel in the little boat again, with the foam pad keeping the wind from our legs, and to resume paddling.

As we rounded a steep rocky point, the three small islands that we knew definitely to be those in the mouth of Rose Inlet came into view. We moved beyond the point, and the wind was then at our backs, the swells diminished to a small chop. We beached the Sport-Yak to empty it for the last time, and to wring out the pad again and stretch our legs. The end, we knew, was only about two miles away, but evening was coming on fast.

A quarter of a mile ahead of us was a large rock, off the end of the last small island. "Just to that rock, Randy, you can do that much." We launched the tiny boat again and continued our slow journey.

Randy had little strength now in his stroke with the paddle and I thought that to break the remaining trip into smaller segments would make it easier for him to keep going. He would not have to think of the entire two miles all at once.

As we drew abreast of the rock, I said, "Now the point on the other side of the channel, just to that point." But it was evident that I was trying to get him to expend energy he simply did not have. Soon I had to skip every other stroke to keep from turning the punt in his direction. His paddle would go forward and enter the water, but he was pulling it back so slowly that the breeze on our backs was about all that kept us moving.

We approached the point that shielded the inner harbor from our view and paddled slowly around it. Now we could see the grove of trees that hid the cabin, one and a half miles away. Everything was snow-covered, white, silent; there was no smoke.

"We can make it that far, Randy. The CB is there. It won't make all that much difference. Somebody from Hydaburg can skiff out in the morning and pick the girls up. They'll be okay tonight."

With the end now in sight in the gathering dusk, we started paddling again. Something was not quite right, though. It took a few minutes for it to register. There was a white line across the inlet ahead of us.

"Is that foam on the water?"

"I don't know," Randy replied, "it might be ice. Probably just a slush we can paddle right through."

We were soon to the edge of it. "Oh, God, no. *No!*"

We knew saltwater ice, we didn't even have to touch it—this was too thick to paddle through, too thin to support our weight. "We'll have to walk the beach from here. It's not much more than a mile," I said. I turned the little orange boat toward the steep rocky beach nearby.

It was almost new moon, and, with it, the largest tides of the month. The tide now was quite low, and two-inch-thick ice lay over the rocks, broken and slanted. We stepped ashore and pulled the punt up over the rocks as far as we could, tied its painter to an overhanging tree limb and started making our way toward the distant cabin, over the steep tidal zone of rock, snow and ice, following the path of least resistance.

I soon stopped to wait for Randy and hollered toward the trees shielding the cabin. "Anybody home? Yo! Anybody there?" I knew it was futile; the lack of smoke told the story, but the silence confirmed it.

I reached a place where an eight-foot rock wall blocked my way—sheer cliffs and heavy snow above, ice-covered water below, a small rim of gravel recently exposed by the extremely low tide at its base. I stood at the top looking down as Randy moved up beside me.

He didn't even wait for the question but simply spoke the answer—"Like this"—and lay down on his belly, spread his arms and legs, pushed himself over the edge, and dropped to the small gravel strip, sprawling full length near the water's edge. I made a poor imitation of his acrobatics, but we soon moved on up the beach.

About halfway to the cabin, the shoreline changed to a more gentle slope and the snow became deeper. Even the sheet of ice on the water carried about a foot of the dry powdery fluff.

Randy's feet had again become numb. I would lead the

way, breaking a trail, and then stop, without even turning, to allow him to catch up. When I heard him move up behind me, I would proceed a few more steps.

At one of these stops, I heard him moving the other way. I had to think of how I was going to turn to see what he was doing. I was so tired that these moves no longer came automatically. When I looked back, he was retracing his steps. I could not figure out why until he stopped, bent over and pulled one of his boots from the two-foot-deep snow.

As his feet had refrozen, the swelling had gone down, and they were now slipping out of the boots that Cindy had slit open with the broken glass a week before. His feet were so numb that the only way he knew when he had lost a boot was when he would see a stockinged foot instead of the green rubber.

The snow was deepest—about three feet—at the top edge of the beach, and only about one foot deep at the extreme low water line. I tried to stay as near the water's edge as possible for the easier walking. Once, as I stopped to let Randy catch up, my footing gave way and I was underwater. There was no bottom, but my floatcoat lifted me immediately to the surface. I had gotten out on the ice without knowing it.

Randy stopped and started backing up without turning, then walked to the incline of the beach and looked helplessly at the snow-covered upper beach and trees. There was nothing he could get to help me with.

My first impulse, of course, was to climb out. As I put my arms on the edge of the ice and shifted my weight to them, the ice broke and I was again chin deep in the freezing water. This act, however, lengthened the hole in the ice. I bent my legs up behind me and hooked the edges of the ice with my toes. Then, with my elbows on the ice in front and my feet catching the side edges, I made a quick jump and lay on my stomach in the snow at the edge of the hole. The ice held, and as I lay face down in the snow, I opened my mouth and took a bite, letting it warm in my mouth so my stomach would accept it. I never thought it possible for snow to taste so good.

I scooted on my stomach toward the beach. When it seemed I was a safe distance from the hole, I got to my feet and rejoined Randy.

The cabin sat facing away from us on a small peninsula about fifty feet above high-tide line. A dock and an attached ramp led upward from the beach. As we approached from the rear, we could see, upward through the trees, the peak of the snow-covered roof only a hundred feet away.

"Maybe we could go up this side and save the walk around," I said, and left the beach to climb the hill. I didn't get twenty feet. The snow was more than waist deep, with underbrush beneath it. We returned to the beach. "Good Lord, Randy, what can be thrown at us next?" I asked as we continued to pick our way around the end of the peninsula.

A few minutes later, I was standing staring at the dock and ramp as Randy walked up beside me. More than three feet of snow lay atop them. The planking of the dock was about eye level and in our present condition, there was no way we could get on top of all that snow.

"You did have to ask," Randy said in the darkness. I knew his face would be expressionless.

"It hasn't got us yet, Randy, c'mon"—and I made my way to the lower end of the ramp and stepped under it. I reasoned that with all that snow on top, there had to be less underneath, so I started up the steep hillside by climbing through the legs and braces of the ramp. Soon I was crawling in the snow as the deck of the ramp low-

ered at the crest of the hill. When I could proceed no
farther, I lay on my side, kicked a depression in the snowbank large enough to crawl out into and stood up. Randy
stood up behind me. By stepping on the edge of the ramp,
we could then climb to the top of the snow.

Moments later, we were in the front yard, stepping
down onto a front porch that normally had four steps
leading up to it. I pushed open the unlocked door, and
we entered the dark interior of the cabin.

We were not strangers here, having visited twice in
the past, the most recent time less than three weeks
earlier. We knew the general arrangement of rooms, fur-
niture, stove and so on. With the front door open and the
white world of snow outside, sufficient light entered to
allow us to make our way about, though the twilight was
now gone and it was a moonless night.

Less than ten feet away was the black-iron wood-heat-
ing stove with an armload of split wood and some kindling, paper and matches beside it. I busied myself with
starting the fire, as Randy disappeared into the kitchen.

The dry cedar kindling burned readily, and the larger
pieces of hemlock soon caught. I closed the door of the
stove and found a kerosene lamp on a table nearby. As I
lit it and closed the cabin door, Randy emerged from the
kitchen, munching heavily.

He held out his cupped hand to me and I accepted
what he offered. It was the almonds-and-raisin mixture
he had remembered, and I filled my mouth automatically. But as I began chewing, the entrance to my stomach clamped tightly closed and I opened the door, stepped
across the porch and spit it out on the snow.

As I came back into the yellow light from the lamp,
Randy was again going to the kitchen. There were some
garments hanging behind the front door—sweatshirts,

bib overalls and heavy shirts. They looked so clean, dry and warm that I stripped off all that I was wearing and dressed in them, leaving the soaked, snow-encrusted, stiffly frozen clothes I had worn in a heap in the middle of the floor.

Randy came back with mouth and hands full. "Rolled oats," he said. "Try them, they're good."

"You'd better get those clothes off and warm up. Have you seen the CB?"

"There's some stuff like that in the kitchen," he answered. "I'll go check."

There was a radio in the living room. I looked it over. It was an AM receiver with a twelve-volt car battery attached.

"It's in here on a shelf." Randy spoke from the kitchen. I picked up the lamp and walked around the partition to join him.

The kitchen shelves were well stocked, with beans, rice, grains, macaroni, flour and canned goods all visible. And attached to one of the shelves was the little citizens' band radio.

It had no power source, however; two black wires hung emptily out the back. No problem, I thought. The storage battery on the radio in the other room will do the job.

"Put some snow in the teakettle and set it on the stove, Randy. I'll get the battery and hook this up. We'll soon be squared away."

I set the heavy battery on a lower shelf below the CB, made a guess at the right polarity and connected one wire to its negative terminal. As the other wire touched the positive terminal, there was an audible snap and a spark jumped in the dimly lit corner of the room. *No*, I can't do this now! I thought as the enormity of the consequences for faulty action penetrated my numb brain. I've got to wait till daylight for this so I can see what I'm doing. "Have you found any fruit juice, Tang or anything like that, Randy?"

"There's a gallon can with Tang in it here, but it's less than half full," he said.

I got cups, spoons and the Tang. We pulled up chairs to what we thought would be the comfort of the stove. We could feel no warmth, however. The fire crackled and sang, the stove was hot, we could feel waves of air on our faces, but the cold was so deeply embedded in our bones, and our outer layers were so numb, that our pleasure was all psychological.

The Tang mixed with lukewarm water was heavenly. As I stirred my second cup, I said, "It would sure be nice if the girls could each have a cup of this tonight."

"They'll get by all right tonight," Randy replied. "And they'll appreciate theirs even more when they get it tomorrow."

Our hands started to hurt then, and we had to move away from the stove. I remember trying to fold the couch down to make a bed, and then total fatigue took over and we slept.

FEBRUARY 25

I awoke at first light with searing pain coursing through my hands and forearms. As I tended to the fire I noticed Randy was awake too, rubbing his hands together.

"How do they feel?" I asked.

"They're on fire," he replied.

"Welcome to the club," I answered. "I've got to see if I can get the CB working."

I easily found the necesssary tools, and lifted the back cover from the CB just enough to determine the proper hookup of its power source. I had indeed been wrong the night before and cursed myself for even trying to hook it up in the dark.

With the battery installed, the dial failed to come to life. There was no static when the squelch knob was turned, no click when the transmit button was depressed.

"Damn, maybe I've damaged it." I was beginning to realize that the only help the girls would get today lay in this little black box that I just didn't know enough about. I took the CB from its bracket under the shelf and placed it on the kitchen counter, pulled up a stool and went to work. I completely removed the rear panel to look for any burning or melti.ng that I might have caused.

I was much relieved to find that an in-line fuse had blown. Apparently it was intended to protect the delicate circuitry from just such bumbling as mine. There was no replacement for the blown fuse, but remote living teaches one remedies for such emergencies.

I wrapped the blown fuse in aluminum foil and replaced it. Though the radio would now function as if the fuse were good, its intended protective purpose had been nullified. I reassembled the CB and wired it to the battery. The dial jumped to life, the squelch knob made static and the transmit button on the microphone made the reassuring click from the speaker that indicated all was in order.

I moved my stool over to the instrument, flipped the transmit switch and picked up the microphone to talk to Hydaburg. The channel selector was set at 11, so I assumed that would be the one to use.

Randy came into the kitchen at that time and said, "The girls are at Keg Point. There's a chart on the wall in one of the bedrooms."

"Mayday, Mayday," I began. "Rose Inlet calling any station, come back please."

I waited a few minutes and repeated the call, but got no response. "Maybe no one is standing by on that channel. I'll try some others," I told Randy.

Turning the selector knob to 10, and then 9, I repeated over and over "Mayday, Mayday! Any station, do you read me? Come back if you can."

Occasionally, I could hear bits of faint conversation and would turn full volume and try to break in, but no one seemed to hear. I turned off the set and joined Randy by the stove, grateful for the cup of Tang he had ready.

"Randy, look through drawers, bookshelves, private papers, everywhere. See if you can find the owner's manual for the CB. Maybe I'm doing something wrong."

My hands remained very painful. The outer edges of my little fingers were turning black, as well as the tips of the two next to them. My feet were starting to come to life also, the numbness and dull ache of the past two weeks starting to sharpen. I noticed Randy walking with more difficulty, turning the bottoms of his feet inward and walking on the outer edge.

Water was becoming a problem. The snow was so dry and powdery that a teakettle-full melted to no more than an inch of water in the bottom. Randy found a galvanized washtub on the back porch and put it to use. He would fill it with snow and drag it across the porch and in the back door to the stove. We would then sit by the fire, adding snow to teakettle, pots and cans sitting on top of the stove. It was a time-consuming and never-ending chore. Perhaps it served as a useful purpose for that very reason.

By midday we were wondering if there had been a report of us missing, and maybe a search started. After trying a few more times with the CB, we moved the battery back to the AM radio, tuned it to the Ketchikan station and waited for the news. We wound a clock and set it to the time given, but when the news came on, there was no mention of us.

Any missing person or overdue boat always receives high priority on the local news. The silence about us meant the girls could expect no help from that quarter. We moved the battery back to the CB. Maybe some boat in Tlevak Strait or Cordova Bay would hear us if Hydaburg couldn't, so I continued calling, "Mayday, Mayday! Any station, can you come back?"

After dark that evening, Randy was searching through the bookshelves, still looking for the owner's manual. "Is this something that will help?" he asked, handing me a small pamphlet. It was the manual for the antenna booster.

"At least it's something to check on," I answered. "But keep looking for the one for the CB. That's what I would really like to have . . .

"The antenna booster!" Suddenly a switch flipped and a light went on in my numb brain. "Of course it can't work, Randy, the antenna is snowed under." Why had it taken twenty-four hours for that idea to come through? How could I be so dense when it was so crucial for the girls that I think clearly? "I'll get up on the roof first thing after daylight and clear the snow away from the antenna. I hope the girls can hold out one more night."

The wind moaned in the treetops above the cabin. It remained cold, and snow continued to fall.

Randy was moving with even more difficulty now, trying to support his weight by reaching for chair backs, the countertop, couch arm, anything to keep his feet from receiving the full weight of his body. With an exaggerated bow to his legs as he tried to walk on the edges of his feet and support himself with his arms, he looked like an ape moving around the cabin.

We bedded down on the davenport for a night of fitful rest. Randy moaned and shouted as his pain broke through his sleep. There was no way I could turn or position myself to escape my own steadily increasing pain. The hospital and some pain-relieving drugs were what we badly needed. Maybe tomorrow.

## FEBRUARY 26

The long miserable night was finally ended by a gray dawn. It was still snowing lightly. I built up the fire and had my first cup of Tang. Randy had been wearing a pair of Jim's white army surplus boots that I put on so I could take care of the antenna. Known as "Mickey Mouse boots" or "clown shoes" because of their exaggerated size, they were made to be worn over light shoes. Now they just fitted my swelling feet.

Dressed as warmly as possible, I shuffled out the back door and found a six-foot stepladder. The snow was only three feet from the eaves of the house, but there was more than three feet lying on the roof. I leaned the ladder against the snow on the roof and bedded it firmly in a backyard drift. Taking a broom and shovel with me, I worked my way up the ladder and into the snow on the roof.

The antenna appeared to be no more than three vertical aluminum rods protruding from the snowbank, but as I shoveled and swept, cross members and braces began to emerge. It was strenuous work, but I kept at it until the entire antenna and its lead wire were clear of

snow. Satisfied that I had done all that I could, I returned
to the CB to have another try.

I had never owned a citizens' band radio, but for several years I had a marine radio, and I knew that trans-
mitting was a drain on the battery. I didn't know if the
battery we were using was at full charge or how long it
could last, so I decided on a message that I would transmit and go quickly from channel to channel without waiting for reply.

According to the manual, the meters on the antenna
booster indicated that all was well, the dial of the little
radio showed strong transmission and the clicks and
static were all properly in order. This had to be it.

"Mayday, Mayday! Two children stranded on the north
face of Keg Point, east side of Dall Island, in Kaigani
Strait. Can anybody help them? They can't hold out much
longer."

I started at channel 11, progressed down to channel
2, then up to channel 40 and back to 11 again, repeating the message twice as I touched each channel. "Two
children stranded . . . Can anybody help them? . . ."

I left the CB on "receive" at channel 11. As I moved
from the stool toward the stove, I found it necessary to
support myself by leaning on the kitchen counter. Randy
was watching. "Welcome to the club," he said.

"We've got to soak our feet good, Randy. It's beginning
to look like we might be here awhile, and if we don't take
care of them, infection could kill us."

We had tried to soak our feet the day before, but the
water felt scalding hot on them, even when it felt cool to
our hands. There was a small bottle of Phiso-hex germicide containing about half a pint, and we poured a
little of it in the soak water. "It burns like hell, I know,
but if we can slowly raise the temperature of the water

high enough, the bacteria that cause infection won't be able to live in it. Let's try to soak our feet at least twice a day for one hour, and the hotter the better."

My feet were rapidly becoming much worse. The frozen parts had turned black, the rest a cherry red, with varying shades of blue interspersed. When I stood on them, the bottoms felt as though they had been run through a meat tenderizer. Every cell exploded. The swelling kept increasing. Pain mounted with the swelling and coursed through feet and lower legs. Since my rheumatic problems began, pain and I have been constant companions, but never had I known anything like this. We had aspirin available, but it served only to irritate my already troubled stomach and had no effect on the pain at all.

My stomach was improving steadily. I found that by chewing a small amount of food well, I could mix it with a swallow of Tang and sneak it into my stomach without its being rejected, and I made nearly a full-time job of eating.

Randy was doing a tremendous job, on feet that must have hurt as much as mine. He had to wade through snow to the woodshed and split wood to be carried, tossed, slid, rolled or in some other manner gotten to the stove. The tub was forever running out of snow and requiring his physical attention. He never complained, just bundled his feet into the big "bunny boots" and hobbled off to do the work.

I asked him to fix up some toilet facilities on the back porch, and he provided a low box for us, similar to a cat's scratch box. After a while, the four-inch step down onto the back porch, the impossible position, the accompanying cold and the step back up to the kitchen were more than I could endure, so he got a five-gallon plastic bucket, put a garbage bag in it for a liner and set it in one of the unused bedrooms. We covered it with a piece of cardboard, and that was the toilet for the remainder of our stay. The outhouse might as well have been on the moon. It was completely out of our range.

As Randy and I began to feel overwhelmed by the futility of trying to get help for the girls via the CB, and as thawing feet incapacitated us to the point that we were hard pressed just to care for ourselves, I thought of another possibility.

We had found two battery lanterns in the cabin, one without a battery at all and the other quite weak. In a kitchen drawer near the sink we found an extra battery, which proved to be fresh and strong. After dark, about the third night at the cabin, I tried shining the strong beam of the lantern across to the steep snow-covered mountainside one-quarter mile from the front of the cabin. The beam reached the white wall, and I practiced flashing *dot dot dot dash dash dash dot dot dot*. The light shone out clearly in the dark night. The SOS signal would be in full view of any boat that might enter Rose Inlet and be stopped because of the ice. It might also be seen from a low-flying airplane. We listened for the sound of engines and kept the lantern on the floor by the front door but never had occasion to signal with it.

A plane could fly over during daylight hours and see nothing out of the ordinary. There would be smoke from our fire, but the chance that the pilot would know that the owners were away was very remote.

We gathered all the bright red and orange things that we could find: sweaters, life jackets and pieces of colored plastic. Randy took them out into the front yard and placed them on the snow. The idea was to make the cabin appear odd enough to warrant closer investigation.

Many times Randy had to go out and take the red things from under new-fallen snow and place them in full view again.

But no planes flew over while we were there, either by day or night.

About dark, as our third night at the cabin approached, I made my way to the damned CB again and sat on the stool. With my voice breaking with emotion, I again made my plea to the forty channels.

"Mayday, Mayday! Two children on the north face of Keg Point . . ."

We then moved the battery back to the AM radio to see if there was any indication that our transmissions had been heard. There was not. They only broadcast irrelevant trivia. We turned it off and went to bed.

It was soon obvious that I would not be sleeping this night, or, as it happened, any of the nights and days that lay ahead. Rather than disturb any rest that Randy might get, I pulled a mattress from a single bed in one of the bedrooms and moved it to the living room floor, as any of the rooms away from the stove seemed freezing cold. I got nice soft blankets and pillows, made my bed perfectly, even tried elevating my feet and legs with the pillows, but the pain was too much. I had to get up and move around by leaning my weight on my hands. So I kept the fire going, ate, drank Tang and hot chocolate, cooked or soaked my feet. I tried to keep my mind away from Keg Point, but it was not possible.

Days and nights started stringing together serving only as an endless conveyer of pain. The days were easiest, since Randy would be awake and we would talk some; the nights were hell.

I grew to fear and even hate the bed. I would lie down when I could no longer sit up, checking the clock as I did

so; sure and steady, it was the only thing I could depend
on. As soon as I was down, I would drop into a delirious
nightmare. I would crawl shouting out of the bed and
look at the clock again: five minutes would have elapsed
and I would get up and try to find something to do.
There were three demons, and whenever I would lie
down, one of the three would get me. The first consisted
of heavy, dark, metallic waves. They would come rolling,
folding and hissing, toward my prone body. As the first
wave would reach my feet, it would smash them with its
smooth weight, the next one would fall on my ankles
and the one immediately behind would fold and fall forward on my lower legs. Unable to stand the pain, I would
cry and crawl away, waking up out of the bed on the
floor.

The second demon was in a mine tunnel. The tunnel
was poorly engineered and constructed, not quite high
enough to stand in, and curving from side to side as well
as wandering up and down. I never learned if the demon
was animal or machine. It made sounds and movements
that could indicate either, but I never saw it clearly. I
would be crawling up the dark tunnel on hands and
knees, and it would catch me from behind, growling and
thumping. It would either bite or grind my feet as I hurried to try to escape it. I never eluded it while staying in
bed.

The third one was a big icy ball. It would roll up to me
as I lay on my back. Bigger than a house, with trees
and rocks embedded in it, rolling slowly, freezing cold, it
would advance to my feet and crush them as I tried to
push it back. As it moved onto my ankles and legs, I
would wake up crying, pushing, crawling—anything to
get away from it.

Often when I would wake up, Randy would be watching helplessly. I would explain to him which demon had me that time, and he would go back to sleep, but I knew from watching and listening to him that he wrestled with a few devils of his own.

## FEBRUARY 27

I was sitting by the stove, probably the third day, cooking a pot of beans, when Randy came from one of the bedrooms. "Look what I found," he said, and displayed a set of kayak paddles. I was unimpressed until he unlocked them from the aluminum tube that held them together, put the paddle ends under his arms, leaned forward, grasping the shanks and placed the handle ends on the floor. He grinned broadly as I realized that he now had crutches to help him walk. "There's two sets," he said. "We each have a pair."

They certainly worked a lot better than the way we had been getting around. I used mine so much that I had to pad the paddle ends to keep them from cutting my armpits.

One day, I'm not sure which—probably just before the fourth night there, we had listened to the evening news and there was still no mention of us—I put what I was thinking into words.

"Randy, we've got to do something. We can't just sit here and let the girls die. It's getting close for them now."

He didn't speak for a while, and then he muttered something I couldn't understand.

"What did you say?"

"Suicide," he repeated, showing more emotion than I had seen him display for years. "You talk of going back to Keg Point when you can't even walk across the room. You can crawl out there on the beach and die, but what good is that going to do anyone? We couldn't even get halfway back to where we left the Sport-Yak, and with the big tides and more ice it won't even be there anyway. Remember those rocks we fell down over? We wouldn't stand a chance of getting back up them now."

He had thought it all out and knew the futility of our trying to get back to the girls. I find it impossible to describe the helpless frustration that I felt at the time. Randy showed it also, but he was right. There was nothing we could do to help them.

There was an indoor-outdoor thermometer on the wall in the living room. We both checked it regularly, more from the want of anything else to do than from concern for the temperature, which usually stayed between fifteen and twenty-five degrees Fahrenheit. Once after I had noticed Randy looking at the thermometer twice in five minutes, I asked, "How's it doing?"

"What?" he answered.

"The temperature."

"Oh! I didn't notice," he said.

He had looked at the thermometer, but his mind was seven miles away by air, a little farther by boat—a million, for all the good we could do.

## March 1

After our fifth night in the cabin, I said, "I don't think they could have made it through last night, Randy."

"I was awake most of the night too. The wind blew all night, and it was awful cold."

"I think the best thing we can hope for them now is that they both die the same night," I said. "The worst thing I can imagine is for one of them to wake up and find the other dead."

"Yeah," he answered, "that would be terrible."

Later in the day, Randy said, "Dad, no one is ever going to understand why we didn't try to go back. Anyone can look at the chart and see that it is no farther from here to Keg Point than it was from Keg Point to here. They'll think we didn't try."

"Just be sure that you know it, Randy. Get it all thought out good and be satisfied in your own mind, then never try to explain it until you can tell all the circumstances. Some people will judge us and second-guess our actions in the summertime when they sit comfortable, well-fed and healthy. Keep in mind that what we did was without benefit of twenty-twenty hindsight."

As the swelling in my feet reached its maximum, it was hard to recognize them as such. My toes protruded black and splayed wide, like tits on a balloon. My ankles appeared only as dimples in the sides of an overstuffed sausage.

I would sit by the stove with my feet in the plastic dishpan, starting with water of a temperature that my feet could tolerate. I would then add hot water slowly, but with all the trying, I could never endure it to be more than lukewarm.

The Phiso-hex was being used up too quickly, so we altered our method. We used dishwashing liquid in our soaking water and applied a small amount of the germicide directly to the open sores after we had patted each foot dry, then we wrapped it in paper towels and stretched a wool sock over it.

The bottoms of my feet had become too painful to bear weight and my feet were now too swollen to fit into any shoe or slipper, so I devised special footgear. There was a remnant of blue carpet on the floor, in front of the bedroom door, that we crossed to get to our toilet bucket. I had noticed each time I stepped on it that it was softer than any other in the house. I cut two pieces from it eleven inches square and threaded string through holes I punched in the edges, so that I could tie one line around my ankle and another above my toes. I then cut two more pieces, four inches wide by eleven long, and used them as insoles to double the bottom thickness.

Tying them on, with the fuzzy side in, made moving about a bit less painful. They became my "carpet slippers."

We found a surgeon's scalpel in a dresser drawer, and I honed its edge. We then used it to cut away dead pieces of skin and flesh on our feet to expose the festering inner layers to the soaking water and germicide. Randy worked at his big toes till bone was exposed. I removed nails and nail beds, the side of a big toe and sections from the bottom of my right foot. The removed skin and flesh was dead, so there was no additional pain in the process, but it was kind of difficult to do, psychologically.

There were many books available on shelves that covered all the walls, to satisfy a wide range of reading interests. The physical pain and thoughts of the girls kept me from reading any of them.

The children had lived most of their lives without television and movie theaters, and for years without even other children to entertain them. This void was filled mostly with books. We would seek out the small libraries that were within our range and tax their patience as well as their resources with our requests for books. (To make it worse, winter storms and travel by small boat meant that we almost never could return books on a schedule.) Any bazaar, flea market, garage sale or rummage sale that we saw we would search for the five-, ten- and twenty-five-cent books we hadn't read yet. A tattered classic with a ten-cent price tag on it would assure us that a trip to town had been time well spent.

We weren't able to keep a large number of books because of their space and weight, and also because the floathouse was constantly damp. We were always eager to trade books with anyone so inclined. Many times we sorted through our books and donated boxes of them to some worthy cause. We gave them gladly where we knew they would again provide other people with the long hours of study, entertainment, laughs or guidance they had for us.

I was very surprised to read recently that fifty percent of the people of the United States have never read a book, other than school textbooks or the Bible. People living in remote places are readers, probably both from temperament and necessity.

Randy made several attempts to read at Rose Inlet, but he found the outdoor tales and sea stories that usually held his interest difficult to get involved in. Cindy and I had read Michener's *Centennial* the previous fall, and we often talked about it. Randy had planned to read it but just never found the time to tackle such an enormous book. It now held his interest better than any of the others on the shelves. I don't recall what was wagered, but I offered to bet that we would be out of the cabin before he reached the end. He took the bet. If I could only remember its terms, I could now collect. He has yet to finish the book.

We craved liquid constantly. Our bodies seemed to have suffered as much from dehydration as starvation. The Tang was used up by about the fourth day, the instant chocolate soon after. I mixed powdered cocoa with sugar and powdered milk and put two teaspoonfuls of this mixture in a cup of warm water. We consumed almost a gallon of the powder in this manner as the days and nights slowly wore on.

No inquisition is as merciless as the one honestly applied to self. I knew that, barring massive infection in the dead parts of our feet, my son and I would live. I knew also that it was at the fatal expense of my two younger daughters. The guilt we both felt was thick and oppressive. Randy responded to it with deep, introspective, moody silence. I tried to pull him up from the depths by discussing it and placing the full blame where it surely belonged.

"Don't blame yourself, Randy," I finally said after a long period of silence. "I made the decisions. It has to be every bit my fault. I just want to know where I went so badly wrong. I want to know how I could have kept them alive."

Finally I said, "It was when we split up. We should never have done that. If we had all stayed together, in a few more days we could have all been to the edge of the ice, and the girls would still be alive."

After much thought, Randy replied, "A lot more likely we would all be dead. It looked too easy, anyway. I don't think we would have let you do that."

"It was when we started to plan for others to help us instead of keeping on slugging it out for ourselves," I replied. "As soon as it was necessary for someone to be here, as soon as it was essential that the CB get people to come help us, everything started to go wrong. The minute we left the girls depending on others to help them, they were doomed. We just didn't realize it for a few days. Now they are gone, and we will live, and we're not worth a damn. Yes, there had to be mistakes, Randy. I have lost two kids. That wouldn't have happened if the right decisions had been made."

"They all seemed right at the time," he said after some thought. "But things just didn't work out. Something was always going wrong."

And I thought back to all that had gone awry.

To begin with, I suppose, was the snow that first night out, which made us lose visibility just before we would have seen the Chacon light. That deprived us of the security we usually had in Nichols Bay, Minnie Bay or the Barrier Islands. Then came the storm, so violent and hanging on so long, unforecasted. My miserable flu and seasickness no doubt prevented me from keeping proper watch throughout the night of February 14. Had we only drifted a short way farther south we would have missed Long Island completely and gone into the then-sheltered waters of Kaigani Strait. We had almost reached that same shelter anyway, before fouling the propeller on the boat. Then there was all the food and gear we tried to get ashore, none of it found, not even the knife that disappeared with one violent roll of the *Home*. The steep, rough terrain that made it impossible for us to get together after swimming ashore through the thundering surf when the boat went down cost us dearly in frozen feet. My decision to leave the Cordova Bay side of Long Island, which was more heavily traveled but open to the relentless southeast storms during the winter months, seemed sound at the time, until we were faced with an unprecedented two weeks of cold north wind. We were unable to use the drift piles and forest as we normally would have, because of the heavy snow and our crippled condition. Next came the surprising similarity between the islands just northwest of Keg Point and those in front of Rose Inlet, when viewed from the beach, to the southeast. This resulted in the decision to separate. Then there was the three feet plus of snow and the iced-in bay of Rose Inlet . . . no one home . . . and the inoperable CB.

Such a vast amount on the debit side of the ledger. So pitifully little on the credit. The books just would not balance. Final tally—minus two.

After thinking about it through a sleepless night, I decided that to discuss the disposition of the girls' bodies with Randy might bring some of his deeper thoughts and unspoken questions to the surface where possibly I could ease part of his emotional burden.

I spoke to him of the life force that was their true being, soul or consciousness, which had departed, leaving only their material bodies to return to the earth from where they came. I told him that regardless of what I would prefer to do, I felt obliged to contact their mother and offer her the girls' remains to dispose of as she saw fit. I mentioned that it was a horrible thing to have kept them from her so many years and then to offer to return them in death. But wouldn't the alternative of not making the offer be even worse?

I told him that if handling their final rites was left to my discretion, I could promise him that no self-righteous, hypocritical, fundamentalist Christian religious sect would have the opportunity to use the remains of our little girls as verbal ammunition in a shouting, frightening, ongoing battle with their personal devils so they could carve two more small notches in the butts of their crosses for public display.

The relief valve was opened on my emotional tank, and a searing, venomous stream poured forth on just and well-meaning people. I ended by saying that, should the girls be subjected to a frenzied, devil-chasing funeral, Cindy would probably lie still in deference to the people present, but I was sure that Jena would get up and run right through the wall.

I know now that the anger was really at myself. The pressure had to be released, however, and when I was through I felt steadier, more resigned and capable of coping with the hell of this living nightmare that I felt was still far from over.

## MARCH 5

The constant eating and drinking was improving my stomach so that I could take aspirin. By our eighth day in the cabin, I had slowly increased their number to sixteen daily. I knew from past experience with my rheumatism that this was the largest amount my system could tolerate.

I had grown numb in both mind and body from lack of sleep. I would fumble and drop things that I tried to hold in my hands. I was becoming unsteady on my kayak-paddle crutches. The five-minute intervals of delirium at irregular times were keeping me from the sleep my body demanded. Then one morning after daylight I checked the clock—seven-twenty—and lay down on the mattress on the floor.

I saw two dark spots far down the edge of the ice across Rose Inlet from the cabin. As I watched they moved slowly closer and the color began to show. One was reddish-orange, the other a bright light blue. My heartbeat quickened as I watched in disbelief. Their faces became visible; they were full, round, healthy and their cheeks were rosy from the crisp air. They skipped playfully along on the ice, keeping near the far shore, singing a song from years past that had dozens of verses. Jena stopped and stooped over to examine something on the ice, as she would on a bare beach in summer. Cindy waited impatiently as she glanced across at the cabin. They continued to move toward us.

I awoke with my stomach churning with excitement, my heart racing. I wanted to pull myself to the window and look out on the ice. They had to be there; I had seen them—so real, so solid, so true to life, even in their mannerisms and their voices! I had to force myself to stay away from the window.

After so many sleepless days and nights, the clock was the only thing I could still depend on. I checked it: eight-thirty. I had been asleep one hour and ten minutes. Or was it sleep? I couldn't figure it out. It was too real for a dream, too pleasant for a nightmare, too disturbing for either.

Later in the day, Randy again mentioned how good some bread would taste. I had made pancakes a few times, but we had no bread, crackers, potatoes or other starches to use in our diet. Also, there was no oven. I told him that I would try, but not to expect too much.

In past years of remote living, I had found it necessary to evolve breadmaking into a faster process. The children had to be fed, but many other things required my time also. Three hours was now all the time I needed from the start until we were eating warm bread with margarine and honey, one of our favorite treats.

Flour, yeast, shortening and milk were in the cabin. Having no oven posed the only problem, but I decided that if we couldn't bake, we could have "fry bread." I mixed the ingredients and set the dough to rise in a deep cast-iron pan with a long handle on it. I built the fire up good and hot, and when the dough had reached the top of the pan, I set it on the stove with a heavy frying pan upside down on top of it. I guessed how much time it would take to bake a crust on the bottom and then, by placing the handles together, I flipped both pans over to crust the top.

The result was above expectations. The center of the round loaf was done, and the top and bottom crusts were thick and brown. We had warm bread with butter and honey, and Randy had the peanut butter and jelly sandwich he had been craving for so long.

My stomach steadily improved, the swelling in my feet and ankles began to diminish and the pain decreased. I could sleep for longer periods of time. Finally we experienced the long-awaited weather change. The temperature rose to the high thirties, the wind turned to the southeast and rain began, falling in slanting, wind-driven sheets. The massive heaps of dry powdery snow shrank overnight to soggy patches. The bushes, released from their heavy loads, straightened. Stumps were now stumps again, rocks were rocks and a boat hull would again be recognizable.

Strength was returning, misery lessening, movement becoming less painful. I talked to Randy about the conversation he had had with Jim concerning their other boat. Jim had told him it was tied up by the creek.

With the warmer temperatures and the change of wind, the ice had weakened, broken up and left the inlet. The beach at the bottom of the ramp lay bare.

## MARCH 8

On the afternoon of our eleventh day there, I put on the "bunny boots," dressed warmly and scooted down the ramp on my rear. Easing myself down to the rubble beach, I picked my way through the rusting, disintegrating remains of the old cannery we had seen marked on the map eighteen months before. As I stepped through the worm-eaten pilings and rotting planks of the last building, I saw the boat lying on the beach nearby.

My experienced eye was making evaluations as I shuffled toward it. Fiberglass, built as a sport runabout, its transom was heavily constructed and braced to accommodate a big, powerful outboard motor. Fourteen feet long and too wide and high-sided for good rowing, its bow was covered for the first three feet aft of its peak. It looked like it had once sported a small curved windshield.

Standing beside it, leaning with both hands on its high side to take the weight from my feet, I studied the boat's interior. Some short pieces of old line, a few small twigs and many leaves formed a dark water-soaked mass on its floor. There *was* a floor; however, my hope of foamed-in-place flotation between it and the hull bottom was soon dispelled.

The boat was tied to the first tree at the top edge of the beach, its transom toward the water. Rising tides obviously filled it regularly, and it drained itself as the tide receded. It was heavy, and with its near-flat bottom tight to the beach and the false bottom preventing inspection from inside, I could not tell how badly it was damaged.

I had a lot to think about as I turned away and started the long, troublesome, three-hundred-yard trip back to the cabin.

I told Randy of my find and we discussed it only as a conversation piece, as I soaked my feet and started a batch of bread. He returned to *Centennial*.

The day's activity had taken a physical toll and I had difficulty sleeping that night. My mind was occupied with possibilities for the new-found boat. We couldn't just stay here and rot, and that is precisely what our feet were doing.

## MARCH 9

The next morning I consulted the tide book, a small yearly publication as indispensable in the homes of southeast Alaska as a calendar. Today's tide would be at its highest at 10:55 A.M. I told Randy briefly what I had in mind and needed his help to accomplish.

We dressed for outdoors on this cloudy, threatening day. About nine o'clock we started to make our way up the narrowing beach to the boat. We found an eight-foot length of two-inch galvanized pipe while traveling through the cannery remains, and Randy carried it along with us. We cleaned the soggy mass of leaves and twigs out of the boat. As the tide slowly rose to near its highest point for the day, we untied the line and pushed the hull, using the pipe to pry it backward into the water.

Randy climbed to the covered portion of its bow and, using a small piece of broken board he had picked up high on the beach, paddled the boat back down to the ramp. In the few minutes required to do this, water was already covering the false bottom.

We positioned it so that, as the tide receded, one side of the boat would rest on a rock, leaving the bottom exposed. Two hours later I was able to lie on the beach, poke my head under and have a look. It had obviously been the instrument of destruction for many barnacles and had also been intimately acquainted with several rocks.

"Patching materials, Randy. Any goops, pastes, putties, resins, tars or plastics—see what you can find. Let's have a go at patching this thing." The best that he found was about two pounds of an epoxy-type compound, a two-part mixture requiring heat to make it harden. To work, it would have to be much warmer than our forty-degree day.

Randy had a solution; he brought the kerosene lamp to the beach. I positioned it so that the heat from its chimney would help dry a small area of the hull at a time. Then I applied the epoxy and moved the lamp back to make it harden, and then moved on to another hole.

Randy found one oar and an oarlock and a spruce pole with a small piece of plywood nailed to it that had obviously been made to double as a second oar. We took a piece of heavy wire and, by bending it several times around, improvised a second oarlock.

As we waited for heat and time to harden our patches, I devised a raised seat with fore and aft adjustment from a piece of scrap planking. Then with several one-by-six boards about six feet long that Randy found for the purpose, I installed a raised floor section to keep our gear— and ourselves, if we had to lie down on it—above the wet floor of the false bottom.

We were actually doing something constructive again. The day passed quickly. I was optimistic about the results of our efforts and tied the line from the bow of the boat to the dock so it could not float away with the high tide in the middle of the night.

We took special interest in the marine weather forecast that evening. With clearing conditions, tomorrow would be a fair day.

Randy asked what I had in mind, and I told him that we could take what gear we thought we might need, food enough for at least four days and two sleeping bags. We could go back and pick up the girls' bodies and, even allowing for adverse winds and tidal currents, get to Hydaburg all right. We would probably be picked up as we got to more heavily traveled waters, but we could row all the way if we had to.

I baked a double batch of bread, and Randy sliced the loaves and made it all up into sandwiches. He filled plastic bags with dry rice and put them in a coffee can to cook over a fire on the beach, if necessary. We tried to remember everything that we had needed so desperately during the raft-traveling days and packed it. We started cleaning up the cabin and returning it as nearly as possible to the condition in which we had found it. We were tired, but something had been accomplished. Things were happening again. We slept.

## MARCH 10

The next day dawned clear and calm, but its beauty was wasted for us because of the task that lay ahead. Randy took a load of gear down to the boat as I continued the housecleaning chores. Soon he was back and said something too low for me to understand.

"What?" I asked.

"It's swamped," he said loudly, and with an irritated sharpness. "It's full of water."

"High on the beach?" I asked.

"No, the tide is still all around it."

"See if you can bail it out," I said. "Let's find out how bad it's leaking."

It was almost an hour before he returned, but the boat was floating, temporarily anyway.

"Randy, if you can keep it moving, I'll keep it floating. Let's load up."

As my son moved our packed provisions and gear to the beach, I sat down to write a note. I just could not bring myself to write of the girls and the job that lay ahead, so I committed a sin of omission. After the cabin had been unused by its owners for such a long time, what difference was a few hours going to make in our reported schedule?

Dear Jim, Sondra or Pat,
  We lost our boat in a blow on the south tip of Long Island Feb. 14. Arrived here the 24th in bad shape. Leaving today, March 10, as we don't know when to expect you back. We are using your old fiberglass skiff and have taken mummy bags, clothes, etc.

We will bring these things back and replace the groceries we have used as soon as we can move around. We need medical attention now for frozen feet.

I may have ruined your CB. If so, have it repaired and I will pay the bill.

Elmo Wortman & children
P.O. Box 192
Craig, AK 99921

I put the note on the living room table just inside the front door and joined Randy at the beach. He had our provisions loaded and the boat bailed and ready. He pushed off after I was aboard and then, taking his position on the raised seat, lifted the oars and leaned into the first strokes of a long, hard day.

By the time we had rounded the point and the trees sheltering the cabin were no longer in view, we had settled into a steady routine. I fastened the alarm clock that we had brought with us under the wide curved rail of the boat so that its face was visible at all times but was protected from rain or spray. We had brought a five-gallon plastic bucket and several small plastic containers of various shapes and sizes for bailing.

I found that by keeping to one of the extreme rear corners, I could cant the hull just enough to make the incoming water gather there and so keep a large volume from staying between the false floor and the hull. This meant making a slightly lighter load for Randy to pull. If I bailed steadily at this pool, it would be reduced to a negligible amount after twenty minutes and I could rest ten minutes before I had to start bailing again.

When we were completely out of the inlet and beyond the islands at its mouth, it was time to change our course to head toward Keg Point. The sun was bright, the sky clear, the water flat calm, an unusual winter day.

Randy was glancing occasionally over his right shoulder to the northeast, toward Hydaburg. "We sure could get a long ways up in that direction today," he said. Not complaining, not questioning, just a statement of fact.

I had been thinking the same thing. The McFarland Islands stood out so plainly beyond the flat calm of Tlevak Strait that they seemed easily within reach today, and they were almost halfway between Rose Inlet and Hydaburg— the hardest half, at that.

"Let's clean up our act," I said in reply. "Let's take the girls' bodies with us."

Without any show of emotion, Randy turned the boat to the south.

Not long afterward, as we were abreast of the point at the north of Vesta Bay, not far from the beach, Randy stopped rowing. He had heard the sound before I did, but it was plain now to both of us: an outboard motor, no mistake.

"It couldn't be clear over on the other side of the strait," Randy said.

"Doesn't sound that far away," I replied. "If it really is near us, it will be going to Rose Inlet. Keep looking between those islands, Randy, and if it's that close, you'll probably see it."

He continued rowing, watching closely, but the sound faded and died and we never did see anything.

So we went on toward Keg Point, each deep in his own thoughts. At every opportunity, I studied the beach. If the girls had given up hope of our ever returning and tried to walk out, they would have perished somewhere on or near those tidelands that stretched and wandered so many more miles than we would travel by boat.

Any patch of orange or light blue would tell us the story before we even approached it. But there was no bright color on the beaches that I could see. So I kept bailing and watching; and whenever I glanced at Randy, his eyes were turned toward shore also.

# 7

# KEG
# POINT

CINDY and Jena had remained together under the sail
when Randy and I left them that morning. Cindy lifted
the edge, glanced out briefly and saw snow falling heavily. Then she quickly closed the sail up again to try to
regain some of the warmth that had been lost when Randy
went out. She was totally exhausted but too tired and
cold to actually sleep. It had been a miserable night.

Jena huddled close. Cindy wrapped her arms about her
younger sister, sharing body heat she wasn't sure was
there at all, but it seemed to satisfy Jena. The pad on top
of them was soggy, and there was a steady drip from the
sail over their faces. They listened to the sounds of the

punt being dragged down the beach. Then, except for
the sound of the wind in the trees, there was silence, as
the wind carried a blanket of snow in on them.

All they had to do now was wait, and they did that
without talking, trying to preserve what heat they could
underneath the sail, each just existing, too exhausted and
miserable to think any thoughts of rescue or home. The
three hours we'd said it would take us passed slowly.

About noon, when Randy and I had been gone over
the allotted time, Cindy again peeked out from under their
cover. She knew the wind had been steadily increasing
and, with it, the snow that was covering them.

"We've got to clear the snow off the sail," she said to
Jena. She sat up and drew the sail back off the two of
them. The chill of the wind against her wet clothing was
unbearable. She got to her feet and pulled the sail up,
letting the dry snow fall off the surface. Beneath it was
a blanket of frozen snow that made the sail stiff and
rigid. Before getting back underneath, Cindy glanced out
on the water in the direction Randy and I had gone, but
the view was blotted out by the snow, and the incoming
tide was advancing toward them.

After another hour they were forced to emerge from
the sail again. This time they had to pull it farther up the
beach against the snowbank, because the tide was now
edging toward the bottom of the sail.

"This sure has been a long three hours," remarked
Jena.

Cindy did not reply. All her strength was now centered
on the sail, as she struggled to pull it out of reach of the
tide. Jena grabbed one corner numbly and tugged relent-
lessly at it until her sister said, "That's enough." Cindy
tried to wring out the water in the pads, but there wasn't
enough strength or feeling left in her hands to do the job.
They would be rescued soon anyway.

But the rescue didn't come. The tide was now much higher than it had been the night before and it soon forced them to drag the sail and pads up onto the snow-bank—no easy task. The snow was built up three feet high, and there was an abrupt edge where the previous day's high tide had eaten away at it. It was a slow, steady pull—then rest—then slowly pull some more. As long as Cindy kept pulling, Jena too gave the effort all her strength. Each time Cindy rested, Jena gratefully caught her breath. It took them over half an hour to get the sail where they wanted it—and even then a portion of it still hung over the edge of the bank. Cindy then retrieved the piece of plywood that had been left at the campsite the night before and pulled it up onto the snowbank too.

Satisfied that they were safely above the tide, they again spread the sail and huddled underneath, out of the snow and the wind.

"What's taking them so long?" asked Jena.

"I don't know. Maybe they're waiting for the wind to let up," Cindy replied comfortingly. But her thoughts were not comforting. She too wondered what was taking so long.

"What's that?" asked Jena.

"What?"

"It sounds like a motor."

Both girls sat up and looked out. They drew the sail up around their necks and listened intently.

"I think it's just the wind," said Cindy. But they sat there a long time looking out.

"We've got to pull the end of the sail up," said Cindy finally. The tide was now at the foot of the snowbank, and they pulled and tugged until they had the end suf-ficiently above the water. Eventually, they settled back down under the sail and listened to the lapping waves at their feet. Cindy felt certain the tide would turn soon. All her attention was centered on the waves below them. She didn't look out; she only listened.

Then suddenly the edge of the snowbank gave way and she was in the water—up to her knees in freezing water—and most of the sail with her. Jena let out a shriek as she slid into the surf in a sitting position, the water to her waist. But Cindy, stunned and exhausted, only shrugged. Nothing surprised her any more.

They were a long time getting the wet sail up out of the water and moving their shelter three feet back from the edge. They could go no farther, because they were up against the trees. Cindy knew they were now safely out of reach of the tide. She brought the piece of plywood around to the foot of the sail, laid it on its lengthwise edge and, as I had done at our previous camp, shoved the edge down into the snow to break the wind. But it worked poorly. The wind was stronger than the anchorage, and the board was left lying at their feet.

They slept for a while that night—a cold, miserable sleep. A two-inch foam pad and a single layer of sail was all that separated them from the snow beneath them. The storm maintained its intensity throughout the night. The thin one-inch pad that they laid over them, its end tucked in at the bottom, reached only to their shoulders. Their heads were exposed to constant dripping through the two thin layers of sail. Since both pads were only two feet wide, they were forced to lie as close together as possible, and they still were not able to completely cover their sides.

Cindy dreamed of Randy and me that first night. She saw me slowly walking down the beach toward her, moving gingerly on my frozen feet. I stopped a few yards away and said, "Just take one day at a time, Cindy," and then I turned and walked away.

She yelled to me, but I didn't hear. I continued walking

away. And then Randy was there, no more than ten feet away. He had a fire and was standing there with his back to the fire and his hands behind him, warming himself. Then he turned toward the fire and brought his hands around in front of him.

"Randy, Randy!" she yelled. He didn't hear her, but he didn't go. He and the fire stayed, and each night, for the next three nights, he would be there—just outside the sail with his fire. As long as Cindy kept her eyes closed, he was with them at night, but as soon as she lifted the sail to reach out to him, he disappeared.

The freezing snow beneath them and the constant dripping of the sail above their heads finally kept them from sleeping for the rest of the night. The aching bones, the cold, the wetness, the weakness, the pain in their feet and their hunger were nothing new to them. They waited for daylight. The storm had died down. They were almost certain they would be rescued that day.

FEBRUARY 25

At first light they made their way down onto the beach. Jena had difficulty standing and edged her way along, reaching out for rocks to lean on to take some of the weight off her painful feet. Cindy had not only the pain in her feet to cope with but her knees, especially the right one, had developed pus-pitted sores where her corduroy jeans, soaked with salt water and often frozen, had rubbed continuously since the shipwreck. She walked stooped over, and she too reached for promontory rocks to take the weight off her feet.

They did not have to go far to see around the point, one hundred feet at the most. Even before they rounded the point they could see the islands they had heard me talking about the morning before as being in front of Rose Inlet.

Cindy looked at them carefully. She couldn't remember what the islands looked like when they visited Rose Inlet three weeks earlier. Furthermore, she was seeing them from a different direction. They were approximately a mile in distance from where the girls stood. As they glanced back into the bay, the shoreline looked formidable. The first few hundred yards were navigable along the beach. The bay they were looking into went back about a mile in a rounded crescent shape. It was a rocky jagged beach; there were steep slopes where the tree line met the water, even now, at low tide.

Cindy studied the next point, which would supposedly lead into Rose Inlet. From where they stood, the forest seemed dense. It was about three miles away, if one were traveling by boat. She thought of the point that she and I had traveled the second night after the shipwreck. She was stronger then. She couldn't do it now, she was certain of that. Also, the sail would have to be left behind. And then she had Jena at her side—and Jena appeared very weak. She suspected Jena's feet were in worse shape than hers. They could never walk the beach. Besides, was the first bay Rose Inlet or was it farther up the strait? She wasn't at all sure. If it was that close, Randy and I or someone from the cabin would have been back for them now that the storm had weakened.

They cupped water in their hands from a small stream and drank. They had not had water for over thirty-six hours. They had sucked on some snow the day before, but in the back of their minds they had remembered my earlier warning, "Don't eat the snow, it will cool your body."

A yellow object along the beach caught Cindy's eye.

Slowly she made her way toward it while Jena waited at the point. It was a small yellow bucket, the kind found in grocery stores at Eastertime filled with synthetic green grass and candy eggs. This one was empty and cracked on one side. She carried it back with her. She wasn't sure why she kept it. From habit, her eyes searched the beach for any other objects that might aid their survival. As they backtracked toward the camp, she saw what was left of the raft. It was on its side, and all that remained were the two spruce logs with a crossbar and the plywood on the back. The center of the raft was an empty hole. She still felt confident that they would be rescued very soon and that the raft-traveling days were over. They wouldn't have any need for it.

As they passed the fallen tree they had tied the raft to two nights before, Cindy caught sight of the thermos sitting on top of a rock, well above the reach of the tide, where they had their camp. The matches were there, but she didn't say anything to Jena about them. There wasn't any more wood on the beach for a fire. They had already tried to burn all the small pieces, and the fire was a failure. The gallon container of diesel fuel was there too, but that, she reasoned, had water mixed with it, for when I had squirted liquid from it on the fire, the flames had sputtered and died. She slowly brought her thoughts back to the present. Why was she even bothering with such thoughts? Rescue was on its way.

The light snow was turning to rain, and it fell heavier as she and Jena crawled back under the sail. They were both shivering. Their clothes were still wet.

"What's taking them so long?" Jena asked.

"Well, maybe no one was at the cabin."

Cindy reached close to Jena and shared what warmth she had. They both listened intently for the sound of the boat that would rescue them. Jena again mistook the sound of the wind in the trees for that of a diesel motor, but after several false alarms, Cindy was not fooled.

"It's just the wind," she said over and over. "It's just the wind."

As the rain became steadier, the drip from the sail on their faces increased. They tried not to bump the sail; each time they touched it, the drips grew stronger. And then the rain gradually turned back to snow and the temperature began dropping again.

"Boy, this sure is a long three hours," Jena said again.

"Yeah, it sure is."

It was now midday, and Cindy was envisioning all the possible reasons why their rescue had not come. Jena, too, was buried deep in her own thoughts about where Randy and I were. Each of them was afraid to reveal their apprehension to the other. They talked very little. They listened very carefully.

As darkness approached, they resigned themselves to another night under the sail. They wrung out the pads as best they could and made their nest. Cindy sucked on a handful of snow.

"Daddy told us not to do that," reprimanded Jena.

"I know, but it's so wet and I'm so thirsty, it's not going to make any difference."

Reassured, Jena joined her and grabbed a handful of snow for herself. She was so thirsty and the stream was so far away.


FEBRUARY 26

As daybreak arrived their third morning on this beach, it was raining heavily. Jena shook Cindy to wake her. Cindy had been talking in her sleep, yelling, "Randy,

Randy!" Her brother had again visited them in the night with a fire, but he didn't hear or acknowledge them. "Cindy, Cindy, stop it. Wake up," Jena pleaded. Cindy had never been at her best in the morning, but this situation was particularly frustrating for Jena. Cindy was four years older; she was stronger and confident. Jena didn't like to see her older sister half awake and yelling hysterically, but Cindy had always been the more emotional one, she figured to herself.

"Randy was right out there with a fire, he was right there!" Cindy pleaded with her. But already, as soon as she uttered the words, Randy and the fire were gone. She sighed and took a long breath.

The two girls again attempted to wring out their pads and make their nest comfortable. The sky was a very dark gray and rain again poured down—it seemed like no day at all. Cindy suggested they go down on the beach and look for some seaweed to eat. Jena took the yellow bucket, and they proceeded to make their way down among the rocks. Jena had great difficulty standing, so Cindy urged her on.

"People eat seaweed all the time. It will make your stomach feel better."

Jena was unimpressed, but she continued to help Cindy until the yellow bucket was half full. Cindy put pieces in her mouth and said, "It doesn't taste bad. It's pretty good, try it." In fact, the taste was not unlike the leaves of a tree—maybe not bad, but surely not "pretty good."

The rest of the day they remained under their cover, listening. Jena still had trouble distinguishing the sounds of the wind in the trees from that of a diesel motor.

They never bothered to go to the stream again. Jena was so weak, she never left the sail after the third day.

"Today is the twenty-sixth of February. It's Monday," Cindy proclaimed. "Gran will be wondering why we didn't call her on her birthday, but she won't do anything. She'll just be worried."

"Margery has probably called the Coast Guard by now," Jena added.

"No, Margery will just worry too. She won't do anything yet. She'll just think we're out at the floathouse and can't get in to see her because of the weather."

"Daddy said she would yell after three weeks."

"I know, but I don't think she did. I think she'll just wait and worry. Poor Margery, she will be worried sick." They never left the sail the rest of that day.

It was on the third night of their survival on the beach alone that Jena had the first of her nightmares.

She dreamed she was on the sailboat again, in the middle of nowhere, in a huge storm. The windows had been smashed in, the wind was screaming through the pilothouse, the masts were ripped off and the pilothouse was tearing apart. Margery was with them, and she was yelling, "We're sinking! We're sinking!"

Jena woke up screaming and shaking as Cindy pulled her close and tried to comfort her. "It's all right. It's all right." Jena wanted to tell Cindy how horrible the nightmare was, but it frightened her even to think about it, so she pushed it to the back of her mind. She could not sleep the rest of the night, afraid to go to sleep, afraid to dream.

Cindy, too, dreamed that night, but her dream was comforting rather than frightening. We were lying under the sail, all four of us, in front of Goldie's soda fountain in downtown Craig, right on the edge of the road. The Skinnas—the family of one of her best friends—drove slowly by in their car. She wondered what the Skinnas must think, and then she thought they had all been rescued. Somehow they were transported to Craig. She must have been too weak and tired to notice the journey. It was raining very hard.

## FEBRUARY 27

By dawn of their fourth day on the beach, the rain had again changed to snow. "Why haven't they come back?" Jena asked. "Do you think something happened to them —you know, because of the storm?"

"No, I'm sure they made it to where they were going. Probably Jim and Sondra weren't at the cabin, and they are just too weak to come back for us yet."

"But what about the CB?"

"I don't know. Maybe Jim and Sondra took it with them." Cindy knew her last answer sounded ridiculous. Why would they take the CB? She had already worked over all the possibilities in her mind. The first few days during the storm, she feared the worst had happened to Randy and me—that we were alive but didn't make it to the cabin and were on the beach somewhere. (That was the same conclusion Jena had come to, though she didn't share her fear with Cindy.) But after the first few days Cindy took a more optimistic view. She believed we had made it to the cabin, but that Jim and Sondra weren't there and Randy and I were too weak to return for them. We had been walking with such difficulty the last time she saw us.

It was this optimistic conclusion that she passed on to Jena. "We've got the easy part. All we have to do is wait. Daddy always makes it. He'll come back for us. I'll go get some more seaweed. You fix up the bed."

Jena sat up and pushed the sail back. She tried to wring the water out of the top pad, but her hands were too

weak. She watched Cindy struggle down the beach, walking slowly, hunched over, with her hands on her knees.
She looked like a crippled old lady shopping in the
grocery store, the little yellow bucket on her arm.

"You know what I'd like?" Cindy asked.

"No, what?"

"A large choc ice."

"I want a strawberry milkshake. A super-deluxe strawberry milkshake. I wonder what you would put in a super
deluxe? Strawberries, vanilla ice cream, whipped cream
. . . I can't think of anything else."

"I'll bet that blueberry pie has mold this thick on it by
now."

"Yeah." Jena giggled nervously. "Do you think we could
take the pads and walk along the beach? We could walk
on the beach when the tide is out and then sit on one pad
and pull the other one over us until the tide changed."

"No, it would be too hard. We couldn't make it around
those points." Cindy knew Jena's proposal was impossible.
Jena couldn't walk, and Cindy no longer trusted her own
footing. On her last trip to the beach for seaweed she had
been afraid she might fall down and not have the strength
to get up. And the sores on her knees ached constantly.
Each time she changed position, her rough pants scraped
the open flesh. Finally she hit on the idea of taking off
her bra, ripping it apart and padding her knees with it.
The effort was exhausting, but it proved well worth it.
At last the abrasion she had been suffering from her pants
was lessened.

"You know what I'm going to do when I get back to the
floathouse?" asked Jena.

"No, what?"

"I'm going to cook. I'm going to cook all the time. I
can make hamburgers like Daddy makes them. With

onions and ketchup and—you know—some stuff like oatmeal mixed in the meat."

"I'd like some mashed potatoes and turkey gravy with it."

"And we can have lemonade to drink. Lots of lemonade."

In the days that followed their conversation constantly turned to food. Jena decided they would always have a bowl of fruit on the kitchen table and lots of snacks around, like cheese and crackers, to munch on whenever they were hungry.

"When we get back, we'll get Randy a bag of Mars bars," Cindy said. "And a three-pound bag of those little jelly beans he likes."

"Make it five pounds. I like them too. And we should get Daddy a bag of rock candy. That's his favorite."

"I think I should go check on the raft. I'll get up in a few minutes and do that. Maybe we could use it and follow them, somehow."

But Cindy didn't get up and check on the raft. The oars were gone anyway, she reasoned. And it would have to be launched at high tide, which meant she would have to walk through the snow to get to it. Furthermore, she didn't even have the strength now to unbutton her jeans to go to relieve herself. The chill and the effort of leaving the sail was not worth it; survival depended on their conserving their strength and keeping as warm as possible. Starvation was taking its toll.

That night Jena again had a nightmare that made her scream. She was on the sailboat again, out in the middle of the ocean, only it was just the four of us this time; Margery wasn't with us. The sea was calm and the boat undamaged. But we were all huddled in the pilothouse, clutching each other. And then a giant wave, a tsunami, loomed above us and crashed down over the boat.

"Jena, Jena, it's all right. It's all right." Cindy soothed her. Jena screamed, but she didn't cry. She became almost stoical. To sleep now was a very frightening experience for her, and she fought it desperately. Cindy lapsed into her own dreams. They were always comforting. For the past two nights she had dreamed the family was all together under the sail, even Margery. And each night we were lying in a different location, sometimes on a sunny beach, sometimes on a rocky beach. But always we were together and warm and happy. She was beginning to prefer her dreams to reality.

MARCH 1

The fifth morning brought bitter cold, and Cindy woke up again screaming, "Randy, Randy!"

"He's not here," Jena pleaded softly. "He's not here."

"I know, I know. But it was all so real. I could see him so clearly, just like he always is, and it was so good to see him . . . so good to see him."

The day was fairly clear, but high clouds permitted the sun to shine through only in small spots. The girls looked out from their shelter at the islands in front of them. There the sun shone, just on the islands in front. It was the first sun they had seen since they were left behind. Then the sun was gone, and the cloud cover thickened rapidly.

"I think I'll get up in a minute and get us some more seaweed," Cindy said. But it was over an hour before she was able to raise herself. And it was an agonizing journey for her down onto the beach. She picked her way slowly and carefully along the rocks. Jena sat up and watched her treacherously slow progress. She watched each little piece of seaweed go into the bucket.

Cindy paused. She was having difficulty breathing. She had noticed it the day before: she had to pause while talking and catch her breath. A brief wave of panic went through her body, and her heart quickened and throbbed. She felt entirely alone out on the beach, and helpless, too weak to make the return trip back to the sail. For the first time, she acknowledged the reality of the situation. "I mustn't make a false step now. I must be sure of my footing."

She eyed the lower beach in front of her. It was low tide. There might be some limpets there they could eat. But to venture onto the slippery mud flat would be too risky. Very carefully, using all her concentration, she made her way back to the sail. Negotiating the snowbank was a strenuous task. She handed the bucket up to Jena and began the long, slow process of pulling herself up onto the snow. It had been so much easier a few days before.

She had taken to napping a good part of the day. "Wake me up, Jena, if you want to talk," she said. When she was awake, Cindy preferred talking to quiet contemplation, but Jena had grown moody, and it was difficult for Cindy to interest her in conversation.

"When we get back," Cindy began, "we are going to clean out our bedroom. Clean it from the top to the bottom and start all over again. I think we should put our two beds together and make a double bed. And maybe we can get a little headboard of some kind, and have a lamp on each side, so we can read."

"And we can curtain off our area and give Randy what's left," Jena added.

"Yeah, that would be okay. And we can order a quilt for our bed, a nice warm quilt. We can pick one out of the catalog."

"And a big, round, soft, fluffy rug for the floor."

"And we can split up our savings and buy a dresser and the material for some curtains—we could just split everything fifty-fifty."

Jena became enthusiastic about the prospects of redoing their bedroom. She wanted to savor the closeness she was experiencing with Cindy on the beach. It felt so good to be so close. It was a new feeling for Jena. She pursued the renovation of the bedroom, but Cindy had already moved on to another topic.

"I'll find someone to take you to the prom. You can go, as long as someone from the high school takes you. Let's see . . . there's this one guy, he's kind of cute, but he might have a steady girl friend this year. I know another one who would really be okay."

"What about you?"

"Oh, I can always find someone. We can make you a dress in Home Ec. Probably a long skirt and a blouse, so you can wear them separately later."

"A skirt with a ruffle on the bottom?"

"Uh huh, and we can get a Simplicity blouse pattern and make one for you and one for me. We'll need some new summer clothes. You know, my favorite sweater and skirt were on the boat. Remember, the football jersey Cousin Diana gave me two years ago, that was so big for me then? It finally fit just right."

Jena studied Cindy's face in silence. She wondered if her own face looked so drawn and strange, like a skeleton's. There were dark circles around Cindy's eyes and they looked sunken. Each of them had begun to notice their hair was falling out and their gums were receding and sore. Jena feared her teeth were loosening. With the braces on, it would make the situation worse. But they didn't talk about it. Jena often mentioned how much her feet hurt, and Cindy feared her sister's frostbite was severe, worse than her own.

"My feet hurt so bad," Jena moaned. "Stop wriggling your toes and just let them go numb. Then they won't hurt. I just let mine go numb."

Jena no longer asked questions about Randy and me. She lost interest in talking about the prom and dresses and redoing their bedroom. After her two nightmares she would not allow herself to fall into deep sleep for fear she would dream another one. She forced herself to stay awake and listen for the sound of a boat. Cindy continually tried to coax her into conversation, and when that failed she proposed that they say the Lord's Prayer together.

As the days passed, it was becoming increasingly difficult for Cindy to distinguish her dreams from reality. She frightened Jena. The early morning hours were the worst; in the afternoons Cindy would again regain her composure and sense of reality. Each day she would announce how many days it had been since the boat sank, and then one day she became confused. She didn't know whether she had already counted that day. But she continued anyway, telling Jena how many days they had been on the beach alone together, how long it had been since the boat sank. Then she hit on the idea of how long it would be till spring arrived.

"Jena, pretty soon there will be fishing boats out here again. Fishing season starts sometime in the middle of March, I think. And the snow will melt too, and then we can find wood and build a fire."

"But we don't have any matches."

"Yes, we do. They are right where Daddy left them. But we don't have any wood until the snow melts."

"Why didn't you tell me we had matches?"

"Because we couldn't get a fire going now."

"Well, if we've lasted this long, we can last a few more weeks. Don't you think?"

"I think Jim and Sondra might go by here on their way back to the cabin. We could signal them. I'll turn my coat inside out so the red shows, and when we hear a boat, I'll put it on that big rock out there on the beach." It was the same idea—of someone coming by in a boat and spotting them—that kept them from moving their camp back farther into the woods, out of the wind. Cindy wanted to make sure they were visible, and also she doubted if they could find a spot for the sail in the thick undergrowth. Once, about the third day they were there, she had ventured back into the forest a short way, but she quickly decided that it would be a mistake to move their camp out of sight.

MARCH 4

On their eighth night on the beach, Cindy began arranging their bed for five people. Jena watched in alarm.

"There now," Cindy said, "we're all set."

Jena lay awake while Cindy talked in her sleep to Randy and me and Margery.

"Jena! The floathouse is out there. It's right there. They've come for us, and they've brought the floathouse!"

"Wake up, Cindy! Wake up! It's not there. It's not there."

But Cindy continued to talk to herself. "No, they're not there. I'm not going to look. Jena Lynn, they're not there, are they?" Jena didn't answer her. "Jena, talk to me."

"Be quiet," replied Jena.

"But it was so nice, Jena Lynn, so good."

Even in such extreme physical circumstances, even as her body retained only a slippery grip on life, Cindy could continue to experience the heaven she had known here on earth. There is no hell for the dreamer.

## MARCH 5

The next morning, when they were removing the freshly fallen snow from the sail, Cindy noticed some small animal tracks. Jena had to squint hard, and even then they were difficult for her to discern, but for sure they had had company sometime during the night or early morning. Cindy pointed out to her where it had walked up to them, investigated, walked around them and continued on its way. It was probably a mink; there are thousands of them living on these beaches.

Jena felt the first real uplifting of spirit that she had had in days. The beach they were on was not totally dead after all. Other things were alive here, just going about their business. They could too.

One thing that would continually come to mind when their talk turned to food was the waste they had seen in school cafeterias, restaurants, even grocery stores, where fruits and vegetables were discarded while still in edible condition to be replaced with fresher, faster-selling produce. They thought and often spoke of the abundance of food they had seen prepared in affluent households by doting parents for spoiled children, much of which was never eaten. They talked about how little of that waste the starving people in the world would require to satisfy their needs.

The girls decided that a law should be passed, internationally binding, to punish anyone found guilty of wasting food in any manner. Oddly enough, at these times they always thought of themselves as people who were only temporarily hungry, who could sympathize with the poor starving. The starving had only a tiny bit to eat over a long period, while they had nothing to eat for a much shorter time.

As the days progressed, the evidence of starvation steadily increased. Each watched the other's face and body shrink and wither as skin was stretched tightly over bones, eyes sank and gums receded. Jena watched the relentless decline of her sister's appearance and wondered which morning it would be that Cindy would not awaken. She will probably look just as she looks now but she won't wake up, Jena thought. I'll go crazy then. She was sure of that. It will totally freak me out. I won't be able to handle it.

Cindy never allowed herself to picture her sister in death. To visualize it clearly and to dwell on the thought could help make it happen, she knew. She would find other things to think about.

They did not talk about these things. To discuss them only served to make them seem more real. To keep them just in their minds helped keep death on a theoretical or ethereal level and out of their world of real experience.

They decided to get a Bible of their very own and read from it every evening, when things were back to normal.

## MARCH 6

One night, probably about their tenth, Cindy dreamed that she had taken her floatcoat off and turned it around, putting it on backward. She had a reason for doing it that was logical and proved to be functional. It made her coat much warmer. I was with them in the dream, and suffering from the cold, so she showed me what she had done, explained why it worked so much better and tried to get me to remove my coat and turn it around also.

During lucid hours the next day she spent much time

trying to recall why the coat was warmer that way. Everything was real and clear to her except the elusive reason, which she never recaptured.

As their bodies progressively weakened and their minds became more unreliable, their moods became sharper and more fluctuating, changing instantly from high to low, from sympathy to uncaring, from optimism to resignation.

One afternoon, Cindy felt her usual need to talk and tried to draw her sister into conversation. Jena did not want to expend the energy either physically or mentally. She wanted only to rest, numb both in body and mind. She responded sharply to Cindy's efforts.

"Be quiet, Cindy. I don't want to talk."

While Cindy was still smarting from the sting of her sister's voice, it changed to one of pleading.

"Oh, Cindy, will you pick the hair out of my mouth? My fingers can't feel."

Their hands were slightly swollen, unnaturally white, deeply wrinkled, as though they had been submerged in water for days. Cindy had always used a private word to express this look, one I have never heard anyone else use. Their hands were "whimpled." The glass cut on Cindy's hand remained yellow, ugly, unhealed.

Starvation continued its steady, relentless progress and the accumulation of falling hair in their nest became increasingly annoying, getting into their eyes and mouths, sticking to their hands and faces.


## MARCH 7

In the early morning hours, possibly of their eleventh day, Jena saw Randy for the first time. He was there, he was real, he was standing and moving around. She was so happy because it was the first time since we had left so many long days and nights ago that she really knew he was alive and well.

Her return to reality made her mind race in the search for answers, but all it could produce were questions. Where had Randy been when she had seen him so clearly? Where was he now? Why was he gone when his presence was so undeniably real such a short time before? What would happen now that she also had received a vision? Was her mind no more reliable than Cindy's?

She marveled at the fact that she now knew intimately what Cindy had been living for the past week. She tried to put this new experience into her usual purely practical perspective, but could not.

Jena was vitally needed; they both knew it. Her firm grip on reality was all that kept Cindy from leaving the protection of their nest under the sail and crawling to eternity toward one of her warmly beckoning visions. All was well as long as solid, materialistic Jena was there to explain what was real, what was imagining. But now Jena was subject to hallucinations, too.

Cindy intuitively sensed that the end was near. The only earthly conclusion that their present situation could hold for them required the quick return of Randy and me. This must mean that we would be there soon.

She told her sister, "Daddy and Randy will be here tomorrow. I just know it. You have to help me bring them, though, Jena Lynn."

Jena believed at first that Cindy's visions had now extended to the afternoon also, but she had endured too much for the idea to disturb her. She listened as Cindy explained that positive thought was a creative force and that for two people to hold the same convictions intensified its power.

"Just know that they are here tomorrow," she instructed her sister. "Watching for them to come, or wishing that they will, won't bring them. We just have to *know* it."

Jena dutifully tried holding the thought, but she had never had much confidence in Cindy's unseen forces. That evening Cindy was in an optimistic mood and tried to get her sister involved in it. After reciting the Lord's Prayer and all that they could remember of the Twenty-third Psalm, Cindy suggested that they sing a song. It was necessary that she make Jena take an interest in something. She couldn't just let her sink further into disinterested lassitude. She was becoming more like a thing than a person. Cindy tried to pull her sister back. Senseless kiddie songs, school songs, popular songs—none seemed in order. It was divine communion that she seemed to be seeking.

After agreeing on a hymn, with failing lungs producing voices so weak—and so well muffled by the sail and the snow around it—that the human ear could not have detected them ten feet away, they began to sing.

> *"Amazing Grace,*
> *How sweet the sound."*

Perhaps it was heard anyway.

As darkness approached, Cindy began her usual ritual of straightening the pads and sail cover in preparation for the night.

"Shall I make the bed for just two tonight?" she asked.

"Yes, Cindy, just two," Jena replied.

## MARCH 9

Toward dawn after their twelfth night alone under the sail, Cindy was to experience her most moving and vivid hallucination.

The floathouse once again was anchored close to their beach. It was daytime, the water calm, the weather warm and pleasant. Randy and I were on the floathouse as usual. Margery strolled down the beach toward it, her path bringing her near where Cindy lay on the rocks.

In recent years I have done much bottling of food. We had no electricity for refrigeration, and it was the only method we had of keeping some variety in our meat supply, most of which we obtained from the sea and the tidelands. When I could get chicken, turkey, beef, pork, even mushrooms in volume and at prices I could afford, I would bottle them in glass fruit jars, for our use in the months ahead.

Margery was carrying a jar of chicken as she neared where Cindy lay. "We're fixing chicken and noodles, so come on over now, Cindy, and let's eat," she said as she continued toward the floathouse.

Cindy was so hungry, and the food her older sister had offered sounded so good, that she started immediately to follow her. Then she thought of her younger sister at the sail nearby who also needed food desperately. Moving to the sail, she said, "Come on, Jena Lynn, let's go eat."

This was uttered plainly to a wide-awake Jena, who immediately recognized that her sister was having another vision. "Wake up, Cindy, there isn't any food," she replied.

Cindy heard Jena's attempt to waken her but clung tenaciously to her beautiful dream. Why did Jena have to be so stubborn? Why didn't she just follow her into the world that was so much nicer than the sail, the cold and the hunger?

"Yes, there is, Jena. The floathouse is right there, and Margery and Daddy are fixing chicken and noodles." She kept her eyes closed tightly to keep out Jena's harsh reality as she continued to live with a foot planted firmly in each world, trying to coax her little sister into joining her on the other side.

"Cindy, it isn't there," Jena said with a sharpness to her voice that forced Cindy close to wakefulness. "There's nothing out there, Cindy, wake up."

Cindy was close enough to the material world by now to know that Jena was right. She kept her eyes closed tightly and tried to cry, but she could force no tears to flow from her starving, dehydrated body. She tried to sob, but her lungs would not cooperate.

MARCH 10

She was forced to open her eyes to their fourteenth day alone on the beach, their twenty-fourth since the boat sank, the twenty-fifth since they had really had a meal to eat. True to her nature, she tried immediately to buoy up her sister and herself.

"Oh, well, Daddy and Randy will be here today, anyway. Don't worry, Jena Lynn, don't worry."

# 8
## REUNION

As we approached the place where we had left the girls thirteen days before, weak, cold and starving, I thought of a ruse to keep Randy from the unpleasant task of viewing the remains of his two youngest sisters. I did not know in what exact location they might have died. If their bodies were below the tide line, any number of small crustaceans would be feeding on them. If they were higher on the beach and uncovered, predatory animals and birds might have fed on their faces. It was no sight for a fifteen-year-old boy who already had endured so much. I could at least roll them up in pieces of the sail and keep him from seeing, openly, the gruesome loads that he must help me carry to the boat.

"Row us over to that rocky point, Randy, and find a place where you can beach the boat so that I can crawl under it, when the tide is out, and fix some of the leaks that I missed yesterday. We can't make it all the way to Hydaburg with it leaking this bad. I'll go see if I can find the girls."

It was little more than a hundred yards from where the boat touched the beach to where we had last seen them. I moved up the irregular, rocky beach on complaining feet and with a heavy heart. As I got near the exact location, I saw that the sail was about twenty feet from where we left it. They had obviously moved it higher up the beach as tides became larger.

As I approached, two mounds were discernible under its folds. The Dacron material of the sail let the bright colors of their floatcoats show lightly through. I could see that the hump nearer to me was Jena because of the reddish orange; the one just beyond shone a barely visible blue.

"Girls, we've come to take you home," I said in an unsteady voice.

Even if I was talking to objects that had long since ceased to hear, it seemed necessary somehow, like whistling in the dark.

There was no movement, no sound, but as I stopped and bent to grasp the part of the sail covering Jena, the part that was over Cindy virtually exploded. And there was the skin-covered skeleton of what I had once known as my second daughter. The big blue eyes were sunken but shining. The face was smiling.

"Cindy, you're still alive!" I exclaimed in amazement, and pulled the cover from Jena. Her head turned slightly on a body that she could not move. "And Jena, you too!" She seemed unable even to show facial expression, but she nodded her head.

I knelt and hugged them to me, crying, "My babies! My sweet, lovely, stubborn children—you're alive!"

Jena cried. Cindy made happy sounds, seemingly capable of neither laughing nor weeping.

Then I thought of Randy. He was still suffering; he didn't yet know. I stood and shuffled a few steps toward the open beach so I could see in his direction.

He had evidently heard some of the commotion and was moving up the beach, fifty yards away. "Randy, they're still alive!" I shouted. "Hurry! Bring the boat over here." He stopped and looked as stunned as if he had been struck. He took a few steps forward, a look of disbelief on his face; then he turned and moved as quickly as possible toward the boat.

It had become a common practice for me, when confronted with peculiar behavior or an unusual request from the children, to roll my eyes upward and start to recite an overly dramatic Hail Mary. As I stood beside a sizable drift log, I leaned my weight on it with one hand to ease the pressure on my feet. With the other hand, I made a fist and banged the log as I turned my face skyward. With tears pouring uncontrollably and unashamedly down my cheeks, I vowed to the entire world, "I will never say another phony Hail Mary as long as I live. So help me God."

As we waited for Randy to join us at the sail, I noticed Cindy was holding a ball of compacted snow in her hand and was putting it to her mouth occasionally.

"Throw that away, Cindy," I said. "We have a jug of water in the boat."

When Randy reached us, we got Jena to her feet. She could not stand. As we took her between us down the beach to the boat, her feet and legs dragged limply behind like those of a rag doll. We sat her on the bow of the boat, but she could not sit up and slumped to a reclining position. I took the knife we had brought with us from the cabin, and slit the arms of the sweater we had put on her, to cover her naked legs and butt, the first day after losing the *Home,* over three weeks before. Randy went back to get the foam pads. The stench was terrible as I removed her clothing. I have never smelled an animal in any stage of life or death that smelled as bad. Her emaciated body was covered with a rash and with open sores, from below her knees to the tops of her shoulders. There was something that she felt compelled to tell me, as I stripped the rotten-smelling clothing from her.

"Cindy and I are real close now," she said.

"Wonderful, sweetheart," I replied.

"Sometimes, we felt so close that we would just lie with our cheeks together."

Always the independent loner, Jena had never before felt the warmth and happiness that close companionship and interdependency can offer. The feeling was so new to her and so comforting that she just had to tell me about it right away. As I placed her poor naked body gently in one of the mummy bags, I hoped sincerely that this revelation and insight might have some lasting effect upon my little Lion. If so, she would have derived some benefit from her ordeal. Laying her as tenderly as possible on one of the foam pads that we had put on the raised portion of the boat floor, I went back to help bring Cindy down the beach.

Cindy was in high spirits and showing off. She could stand alone. With her feet spread wide apart, her knees bent, back and shoulders hunched over, and arms extended to maintain balance, she was standing, but I honestly believe that she was less than four feet tall. And she could not take a step. Had it not been for her exuberant, infectious spirit, the exhibition would have appeared pitiful.

"How did you do it, Cindy? How the hell did you do it?"
I asked.

"It wasn't so bad," she replied. "We would say the
Lord's Prayer, and that helped, and we could say some of
the Twenty-third Psalm. And Daddy, you said you would
be back. We knew that you and Randy must be having
an awful tough time to be gone so long. We had the easy
part. All we had to do was wait."

Fantastic!

In her hand she still held her snowball. I took it from
her and threw it away.

"Oh, Daddy, why did you do that?" she objected.

"I told you we have drinking water, Cindy. You don't
need it," I answered.

"But it was just getting so that I could get some water
out of it, and I have been working on it all day."

She was definitely disturbed. I was surprised by her
quick change of mood. This was not the Cindy I had known
for the past sixteen years. I was sorry I had brought her
down from her high, though I could see nothing so terrible about throwing away her snowball. Surely, I thought,
it must be the effect of the extreme and terrible situation
she has been in these past few weeks, and she will soon be
back to normal. And, indeed, this proved to be the case.

As Randy and I took Cindy between us and moved her
down the beach toward the boat, she made an effort to
bring her feet forward and assist us, but the result was
negative. Give her an E for effort, though. She tried and
was immediately restored to her usual good humor.

When removing her clothes, I found her body to be as
pitiful as Jena's. It looked as though, had I been capable
of just picking her up and giving her one good shake,
there would have been nothing to keep all her clothes
from falling from her emaciated frame to a pile on the

beach. There just was not enough of her left to hold them on.

As I removed her jeans, her bra appeared in the legs. "Cindy," I said, "did you get so thin you couldn't keep your bra up?"

"Don't you see, Daddy? I took it apart and put the cups on my knees because they were too sore to crawl on to go out on the beach for seaweed."

Randy was just there, physically functioning, useful, but mentally numb, not joining in conversation, not crying, not laughing. He did what he could to help. He kept the boat bailed out and pushed it back occasionally so it would not be solidly beached as the tide receded. He appeared to be in emotional shock. It would have made no difference whatever the weather, but the day was wonderful now; the sky was blue, the sea was calm.

The sail, which had served its intended purpose so well in past years, had adapted nobly to an alien, life-sustaining utility for the past twenty-five days. Only a short hour before, I had envisioned it as a shroud. We left it lying smelly and stained, high on the beach under the trees.

"What food do you have?" Jena asked.

"Plenty," I replied. "Just as soon as we get the boat under way you can have all you can eat." I thought that shrunken stomachs and long-idle digestive systems could only accept a small amount of food at first. What a surprise I was in for!

As I moved to the back of the boat and started bailing again, Randy pushed the bow from the beach, dragged himself aboard, and sat on the raised plank seat in preparation for the task that only he could perform. He questioned whether we would have enough food for all we needed, now that our number had doubled and the girls obviously would make a ravenous attack on our carefully planned supply. "No problem, Randy. We'll go right back to Rose Inlet. These girls need more than just food."

As Randy deftly turned the boat and started his strong, steady pulls on the oars, I reached into our supply sack, got a sandwich and handed it to Jena Lynn. As I got one for Cindy, Jena said, "I can't swallow it. It's just too sweet. She had taken a bite and was chewing with a puzzled look on her face. The sandwich I had given her was bread, margarine and honey. "I can." Randy reached and took it from her, never breaking his rhythm with the oars. I got her a peanut butter and jam sandwich. That "hit her mouth better," as she expressed it, and she began eating steadily.

Cindy ate slowly, sparingly, talking in a steady stream, asking many questions and telling us how they had lived for the past two weeks. She needed emotional release; her mind seemed far hungrier than her body. She was so thoroughly spent that often, while still talking, she would slip into a sleeplike unconsciousness.

After two sandwiches, Jena asked, "What else do you have in that food sack?"

"Plenty, babe," I answered and brought out shelled nuts, raisins, two sacks of popcorn and dozens of sandwiches. I showed her the little bags with rice that Randy had wanted to bring, with the coffee can so that it could be cooked on the beach.

She had to try some of everything. Chewing, savoring, luxuriating. I would see her take a bite and then just rest, without the necessary energy to chew what was in her mouth. She eventually selected the popcorn as being most deserving of her voracious attention and settled into her mummy bag with one entire bag of it. When that was consumed, she asked for the remaining bag and began on it, seemingly oblivious to the rest of the world.

Once, for a minute, as the talk ceased, Cindy said, "The boat sank on February fourteenth—no, it was after midnight, so it should be called the fifteenth," and she began to recount the different moves we had made, putting our entire misadventure into chronological order. On a few points, I was sure that she was in error but did not correct her. Later, however, our detailed research proved she was right. She wanted to know all that Randy and I had been doing, what our circumstances had been. She showed much interest and sympathy as I recounted for her our stay at the cabin, often in emotional sobs as I told how we thought they had died and we had only come back for their remains. She asked if we knew of any search efforts, and why Margery had not reported us missing. I explained that there had been no search. As I had it figured, Margery was in a dilemma. She knew how violent Dixon Entrance could be, and as the weeks passed with no word from us, she would worry and she would suffer. But we would either have to be at the floathouse and well, or we would be gone forever, and as long as she could hold some hope of the first alternative she would not be forced to accept the harsh reality of the last.

"Why didn't you girls answer me when I first spoke to you back there?" I asked.

Cindy said, "I have hallucinated a little bit"—the understatement of the season—"and Jena Lynn would sort things out for me. When I heard you, I looked at her to see if she had heard you too. She didn't say anything, but when her eyes started getting big, I knew you were real."

At one time on the return trip, we heard boat engines. Randy and I kept a steady watch in the direction of the sound. Soon he saw them: two trollers, one behind the other, near the islands on the far side of Kaigani Strait. I could see them now also, moving slowly south. Jena wanted to see, so I helped her up far enough so that her head was above the side of the boat. But her poor near-sighted eyes could not even make out the islands that the two boats were near.

"Can't we signal to them?" Cindy wanted to know. "You can wave my floatcoat with the red side out."

"It would be useless, sweetheart. They're so far away that we can hardly see and hear them. We would be only a tiny speck to them, and so near the beach it would make us blend into the background. Even if they were looking for us, and knew exactly where we are, it's doubtful that we could make ourselves seen. But don't sweat it," I told them. "We're just a few more hours from the cabin, and everything that we really need right now is there."

The sunny afternoon diminished into crisp evening. Randy pulled steadily at the oars, and the boat moved slowly onward. I continued to bail methodically, against the ever-replenished pool in the bottom of the boat. Jena kept on eating, and Cindy never ceased to talk whenever she was awake.

We passed the first bay that had separated us for so long, then the second. The boat was moving slower as we came abreast of and moved on beyond the open north-facing point, where the wind, snow and waves had thrown Randy and me so harshly and unceremoniously ashore in the punt. It was dark as we approached and passed between the islands that had figured in my erroneous decision to separate, seemingly ages ago. Then we rounded the last point of land that concealed and protected Rose Inlet. The group of trees sheltering the cabin was visible a mile and a half away, in the pale light of the moon, behind now-gathering clouds.

The boat had slowed even more. Though the oars were moving with the same steady rhythm, the power applied to them was lessening. I asked Randy how he was doing. "I'll make it," was all he said.

"It's close now, don't strain. Just hang in there, fella." Eventually, the dock was visible with the attached ramp leading upward. The boat ground to a halt on the rocky beach before it.

"We'll never be able to get them up the ramp in these mummy bags," I said to Randy. "Let's go up and get a fire started and fold down a bed, then bring some dry clothes back down to put on them. Will you girls be all right for a few minutes?"

"Everything is just fine, Daddy. Go do whatever you have to," Cindy replied.

Randy and I pulled the bow of the boat as far up on the beach as we could to keep the girls clear of the incoming water, now forced to the stern of the canted hull.

As we climbed to the top of the dock, Randy exclaimed, "Hey! That newspaper wasn't here before." He was right, but it could have been under the snow and exposed by today's thawing.

As the beam of our battery lantern pierced the interior darkness of the cabin, it rested on a jumbled mound in the middle of the floor.

"Groceries! Look, Randy, someone *has* been here since we left this morning."

I shone the light on the table where I had left the note. It was gone. Things were happening too fast. My mind tried to keep up, to get the world into order. It no longer contained just the children and me and our cold, hunger, snow and pain. Others were becoming involved, and it was difficult to adjust my thinking to include them.

I had a fleeting insight into Randy's difficulty in continuing his efforts on the evening that he and I had first arrived at Rose Inlet. When you are physically and emotionally spent, with your goal always promised, ever strived for, but never reached, the mind will limit the world and eventually blank out the end result as being unreal.

The end was definitely in sight now, however. I had to make room for it and force my mind to accept it.

I moved automatically to the chores at hand, trying to look beyond our little world of misery to the conclusion of our ordeal and to the beauty, comfort and plenty that lay ahead.

We returned to the girls with a sweater, bib overalls and a pair of socklike slippers. We moved Jena to the bow of the boat and unzipped her mummy bag, dressing her naked body as it was exposed. We carried her between us the few steps to the dock and, lifting her up, pushed her to its deck like a small bag of potatoes and then climbed up beside her.

Randy had been at the oars for thirteen hours, with a one-hour respite at Keg Point as we cared for the girls and loaded them into the boat. It had been long, hard, grueling work. Now, on feet with bare bone protruding where nails and ends of toes once were, he took his little sister on his back and, leaning forward, carried her surely and safely up the long steep ramp to the cabin beyond. Our strong, enduring, dependable Randy, the one we had all relied on so often, continued doing his thing. He would be all right. I felt great admiration for him.

I followed behind them, unable to keep up. I pleaded with Randy to hold tightly to her because she could not hold to him. I pictured Jena slipping from his back and me unable to stop her tumbling, sliding descent down the dark, frosty ramp to the rocks beyond.

In the cabin, we removed her clothes and placed her in the bed we had prepared, taking the same garments back, repeating the process and bringing Cindy up to the cabin.

"Our situation is known," I told the children. "They didn't find us today, because I never mentioned in the note about going back to Keg Point. But someone will be back here in the morning. We will all be in the hospital in Ketchikan before tomorrow is over. We must get ready."

With water warmed, I began the task of cleaning the girls. Such a pitiful mess. One at a time, I set them on a footstool beside the made-up davenport and with soapy water and washcloth started to cleanse as gently as possible the skin so covered with rash and open sores. As they each slumped over, I leaned them against the bed and continued. When they could not maintain that position, I lay them on a towel spread on the floor, washed the areas thus presented, and then turned them. I washed, rinsed, patted dry with a towel and then applied hand lotion liberally to their entire bodies.

I tried to soak their feet, but, as had been the case with Randy and me, the water felt scalding hot to them, though it was actually cool. I was so thankful that they would be hospitalized and have pain-killing drugs while their feet thawed. They would not have to experience it "cold turkey" as Randy and I had. They asked what I thought of their feet. How bad were they, really? Would they lose parts of them, as Randy and I had already done? I gave them my honest, uneducated opinion. All Jena's toes seemed safe. Her painful efforts in constantly moving, wriggling and flexing them during the past weeks, trying to maintain circulation, perhaps would be rewarded. Cindy's losses would be minimal, I thought. Maybe she'd lose a few nails, but it looked like she'd keep all her toes.

I was concerned about the possible inability of their

long-starving bodies to cope with eliminating the wastes
from the unbelievable amount of food they were consuming, especially Jena. I put raisins in a small pot of
water on the stove and let them simmer, then had the
girls eat the raisins and drink the juice.

When Cindy expressed doubts about this, Randy told
her, "They don't taste bad at all. He had me do it when we
first got here, and they really work." (By morning they
had done their duty for Jena, but it seemed that Cindy
would require dynamite.)

It was 2 a.m. and we were all completely exhausted. I
told the girls that we would just have to wait till morning
to shampoo their hair.

I did not sleep for the remainder of the night. I kept
the kerosene lamp burning in the kitchen so that the living area, where the children were, was in soft shadow.
They had lived through more than enough dark nights.
I kept the stove stoked, and water on top, heating. I sat
by the fire or moved about on the kayak-paddle crutches,
slowly unwinding.

Whenever I glanced at the couch with its light, pre-
cious load, Jena would be awake, smiling, watching. She
would be fondling and stroking the blanket that covered
them, completely captivated by the clean softness that she
could now feel, smell, savor.

About 4 a.m. I asked softly, "Can't you sleep, love?"

"I'm not sleepy, Daddy, just hungry," she whispered.

So I made even further inroads into the well-calculated
fresh grocery supply that we had found on our return, a
supply probably intended to last for months. I peeled some
potatoes and diced them into a pot of water on the stove,
adding an onion, some dried green pepper and various
seasonings as it simmered. When the potatoes were thoroughly cooked, I let the pot cool slightly and turned the
broth to milk with the powder that was there. I was thor-

oughly amazed that Jena could consume it as though she had eaten nothing the previous afternoon, evening and night.

## MARCH 11

The other two children awoke to the pleasant aroma now filling the cabin and joined in this early, impromptu, unconventional breakfast as the first weak evidence of approaching dawn slowly lightened the sky for Sunday, March 11.

Randy fixed a garbage-bag five-gallon-bucket toilet and placed it near the girls' bed. They still required some assistance in moving onto it and then returning to the bed, but much of their rash had disappeared during the night and they were noticeably stronger.

Their hair, however, smelled strongly of the conditions we had found in their nest at Keg Point, so in the light of full day I shampooed and dried Jena's hair. We were not hurrying, just slowly moving, relaxed, enjoying life and each other. Then, we heard the kind of sound we'd been listening for, waiting for, hoping for, for so many days.

# 9
## RESCUE

"HELICOPTER!" shouted Randy. The throbbing sound was unmistakable as it reverberated along the steep canyon walls of Rose Inlet. Soon the aircraft hovered in full view of the cabin: the big, slow old chopper referred to with rude affection by Coast Guard personnel as the "flying shithouse." Cold, noisy, powerful, requiring a five-man crew but loaded with sophisticated electronic navigational equipment, it was on call for the most hazardous rescue missions anywhere in southeast Alaska, any time, any weather.

We learned later that search efforts had been made the previous day. The helicopter, based in Sitka, had been low on fuel as it began today's search. But before going to Ketchikan to refuel, the crew decided to check the cabin at Rose Inlet, where we were last reported. As they approached the cabin, the boat we were known to be using was seen tied to the dock, lying awkwardly on the beach.

They had us. It was over.

"Cindy, I will not let you go back to civilization with your hair looking and smelling like that," I said. Putting some water in the plastic dishpan I went to her, bent her head forward and wet her hair. "There, I am washing your head, and they will just have to wait until we have finished."

As it happened, we had plenty of time. The crew had difficulty finding a safe landing place for the big helicopter, finally settling on a grassy tidal bar at the mouth of the small stream a quarter mile away. Soon two helmeted Coast Guardsmen with walkie-talkies climbed the ramp. We opened the door, and they entered.

"Are you Elmo Wortman?" one of them asked.

"I am."

"Are you ready to go?"

"We are."

"You didn't get far yesterday, did you?"

"We got a *long* way," I replied. "But that story can wait."

Surveying my pitiful little crew, one of them suggested getting the chopper airborne and lowering the rescue basket in the front yard. The other fellow thought not, because of the danger of operating it so near a tall spruce tree that grew nearby.

"Can you walk?" he asked.

"The girls can't, but they're not very heavy," I replied.

Jena, with twelve-year-old vanity, was very glad at that moment that she was clean. It was such an improvement over her condition for the past days and weeks that she took no notice that the clothes she wore were men's rough outdoor garb and could easily wrap twice around her small emaciated body. Her hair was shampooed and combed. She was very impressed by the tall, strong Coast Guardsman with the soft southern accent who was so courteous and attentive to her and who wore the pleasant scent of recently applied cologne.

He took her in his arms and carried her gently from the cabin. He let her hold his helmet and walkie-talkie. He even called her "Ma'am."

So that is how we left. The last one out of the cabin, I looked around at the mess we were leaving and thought of the neatness and order we saw when we first arrived. As I closed the door, I hoped Pat Tolson would understand.

# 10

# LOOKING BACK

WE later learned that Pat had been concerned that the cabin was vacant for such a long time and returned to it as soon as he could, on March 10. He saw my note on the table and read it and realized that it was dated March 10, that very day. It was only 11 A.M. He felt the stove, and it was still warm.

My note was then put to a use for which it was never intended. I had meant it to explain the food we had eaten, the wood we had burned, the clothes and gear we had borrowed. He applied it as an instrument for effecting our rescue. When used with that intent, at that time, it was misleading.

If we had left Rose Inlet that morning to travel to civilization, as my note indicated, we would have gone northeast toward Hydaburg. Returning to Keg Point for the bodies of the girls, which I had not mentioned, placed us not on that course, but to the south, almost in the opposite direction.

Pat had just come from Hydaburg on the same course that we would have taken to go there. He had not seen us, but he was thinking only of his home and returning after a long absence. He thought that perhaps he had passed us without noticing.

For the return trip he lightened the load in his skiff by throwing his groceries quickly into a pile on the cabin floor and, taking the note with him, sped out to look for us, going north from the mouth of Rose Inlet while Randy and I rowed south.

As Pat entered the broad expanse of Tlevak Strait, he tried to put all possibilities together to pinpoint an area in which he would find us. The tide would soon be at its highest level for the day. The currents in Tlevak Strait could not yet have had an adverse affect on our course and pulled us to the south. He knew the condition of the boat we had. Had it sunk, and us with it, in open water? Had we managed to get to one of the many islands along this course, and were we presently stranded on a beach? Was the boat now sinking and so low in the water that it was hard to see?

By early afternoon, Pat met a larger boat and told the crew of our plight. The information was relayed to Hydaburg by radio and more boats and people joined in the search. The two trollers that we had seen on our return to Rose Inlet with the girls were, in fact, searching for us. Hydaburg's residents notified the Coast Guard and they also called Craig to report the incident. They found out about Margery and called her. The Ketchikan Search and Rescue Squad was also notified.

During the night some of the boats continued to search

in the hope of sighting a fire on a beach on one of the many islands. The work was also done to prepare for a massive, coordinated search to begin at dawn. We will forever have a warm spot in our hearts for those wonderful caring people who put so much effort into trying to find us, that day and part of the next one also.

After the Coast Guard helicopter had us aboard and flew out of Rose Inlet to where radio communication was better, the crew contacted Matthew Carle, who heads the Hydaburg Search and Rescue Squad, and told him that we had been located and were on our way to Ketchikan General Hospital. Many of the smaller boats involved in the search did not have radios and continued their efforts throughout the day.

Of all the frustrations of those weeks, not being able to get the CB to work was one of the most ironic. Yet the Cordova Bay area is notorious for its poor radio reception. It is common for boats in the vicinity to be reported missing because radio contact cannot be made.

On February 7, when we had visited Jim and Sondra at Rose Inlet, he mentioned that they had a CB radio and talked to Hydaburg. We assumed they did so at will. Because no one could predict that we'd need such technical knowledge, he did not say that they could use the CB only at about 10 P.M., and only on the nights of best radio reception.

Another factor I have to look back at is my faulty decision that we should separate. In retrospect, I now see that although it was based on a miscalculation in our location and resulted in a very difficult time for all of us, it might possibly have been the key factor in our survival.

Within three days after Randy and I had left them, the girls were too weak to travel. Jena never stood or left the sail after that time. Cindy's movements were limited to less than a hundred feet, and even then she was afraid of not being able to return to the sail. If Randy and I had stayed with them and we all declined to that physical condition, it is pure speculation as to how long any of us could have lived. No one would have known our location or even been looking for us for some time.

The storm itself had been of terrible power. In the hospital I was visited by a Coast Guard officer who asked many questions, one of which was, "How strong were the winds in the storm of February fourteenth?" I told him that they were over fifty knots, but that we had no wind gauge so I couldn't say exactly. In his official report, he wrote that the winds were forty knots.

A tugboat captain sent word to me that the Coast Guard was in error on their reported wind velocity. He said he was in that storm also, and that the winds had varied between seventy and eighty knots (eighty to ninety miles per hour). He also sent a picture of his ice-encrusted tug that was taken after they had passed through the storm.

Within a year of our experience, there were more than forty people that I know of dead or missing in the violent waters of Dixon Entrance. Thirty of them were aboard the Taiwanese ore carrier *Lee Wang Zinn*, which apparently turned over within five miles of where we were first forced to sea anchor. Alaska Outport Freight Service lost a large barge in heavy seas near the entrance to Cordova Bay, where we lost the *Home*, and with it were lost winter grocery orders and Christmas purchases for many people in the remote communities of southeast Alaska.

There is no simple reason why Cindy, Randy, Jena and

I are not on the list of dead or missing. Each person who knows anything about such matters can find a reason that parallels and supports his personal convictions. Paul Breed, former Coast Guard commander, bush pilot and present airline owner, who has known us for several years, was quoted as saying, simply, "If any family could survive it, they could."

My own theory also has to do with the background of our family. The children and I know the beaches of British Columbia and southeast Alaska as intimately as families living in town know their front lawn and sidewalk. We have lived on or near them for many years. Several times in the past when traveling about in our "water world," miles from home, we have encountered storms with winds so strong we could not get back. We would pull our skiff to the beach, turn it upside down with its back to the wind and the other edge propped up, build a fire in front, crawl underneath and wait for calmer weather.

One summer, when Cindy and Jena were twelve and eight, they asked me to take them to a small island, miles from home, to spend two days and nights alone. They took a blanket, a six-foot-square piece of plastic sheeting, a knife and a few matches.

They built their plastic shelter, gathered wood and started a fire. When the tide went out, they found their food and prepared it. Their neighbors during this time were the wolf, bear, wolverine, mink and deer. I felt they were safer than if they had been among the more violent and unpredictable two-legged animal species. When I returned to pick them up they were laughing, well-fed and confident. They had spent a most enjoyable weekend.

I have tried not to restrict the children in their choice of games, but just point out to them the potential dangers involved. They would climb the mast and sit on the cross-tree when we were under sail. They would swing in the rigging. They dived from the roof of the floathouse and swam in the frigid north-coast waters, both intentionally and accidentally. They explored steep cliffs and deep caves. They skated and played on the saltwater ice around us in winter. They were gaining experience, poise and confidence that would prove invaluable to them, but I do not believe that they lived in any more danger than the child who rides a bicycle in an urban neighborhood.

As for me, when I lay down to die after we were wrecked, Cindy and Randy picked me up and made me go on living. When, because of my error, the girls were left alone for so long, they hung on, took care of each other and lived. In so doing, they made the balance of my life worthwhile. I had a good crew for the *Home*'s last trip, a hell of a good crew.

# Epilogue

THE results of our experience have been different for each of us. What do the children now say about it? "A real 'bummer' of a trip, but no big deal."

Randy had allowed his toes to thaw as early as February 15 while tending night fires. Though they had refrozen on February 24 as he and I made our way to the cabin, they were thawed again soon after. When we reached the hospital on March 11, his feet were in stable condition and ready for surgery. He was hospitalized only four days before returning to Craig to stay with friends and enter public school.

Jena was fortunate to spend that first night on the beach with her feet up under Cindy's coat. In that way she escaped the frozen feet that Cindy, Randy and I experienced. Her constant moving and flexing of her feet over the next three weeks, though painful, kept her from losing toes or having skin grafts. She was hospitalized for two weeks to recover from her starved condition, before returning to Prince of Wales Island to stay with friends and enter school.

Cindy's feet were still frozen when we reached the hospital. She remained there three weeks while having surgery on three toes, skin grafts on her feet and recovering from malnutrition.

I was hospitalized for three-and-a-half weeks. The front half of my right foot was amputated, as well as all the toes of my left foot (in varying amounts). I will never have to trim my toenails again.

We moved the floathouse into Craig as soon as we were physically able, and the children attended public school. All correspondence-school books and materials had been lost with the sailboat, and those studies were never resumed.

Randy and Jena had the braces removed from their teeth on the next visit to the orthodontist. Cindy's dental work was completed before summer vacation was over.

Six months after our ordeal, the three younger children were back in school here on Prince of Wales Island; Margery, who had been valedictorian of her high-school graduating class, entered Eastern Oregon State College at La Grande. Randy participated in track and wrestling, Cindy in track and volleyball. Though the skin grafts on her feet still give her some discomfort, Cindy paints nails on her toe stubs and continues to run.

Cindy was fortunate to be one of two students sponsored by her French class to spend six weeks in Europe during March and April 1980: five weeks in Marseille, with visits to Italy, Switzerland, Paris and London.

Jena received the award for Highest Academic

Achievement in her eighth-grade graduating class in June 1980.

As we returned to a more normal life style, their personalities also returned to normal.

Cindy still gets totally involved in the lives of others and remains absentminded about her own affairs. She misplaces such things as the mailbox key, her contact lenses and the plug to the bathtub.

Randy is in just as big a hurry to live all of life as any other normal sixteen-year-old boy. He has two skiffs and an interest in a third, with no time to do the necessary maintenance and repairs on them, but he *needs* a larger boat, a better boat, a car, etc.

"Yes, Jena Lynn, the election you lost was probably controlled to the point of being no more than an appointment, but make your bed and pick up your dirty clothes; that is something you can do right now to benefit the entire world."